The Daily Telegraph

Caring
for loved ones
in old age

0

counsel + care

for older people,

Caring for Loved Ones in Old Age
by Counsel and Care

First edition 2007
  Reprinted 2007

Copyright © 2007 Counsel and Care for the Elderly

Lawpack Publishing Limited
76–89 Alscot Road
London SE1 3AW

www.lawpack.co.uk

ISBN: 978-1-905261-49-9

Exclusion of Liability and Disclaimer

Contents

About the author

Counsel and Care is a national charity getting the best care and support for older people, their families and carers. It works with older people and their carers to ensure that they are aware of, and receive, their rights and entitlements, and promotes choice and control in later life. The charity operates an advice service which deals with around 100,000 enquiries per year, through telephone calls, emails, letters and the website. Counsel and Care also publishes a large range of fact sheets for England, Wales and Scotland about all aspects of the community care system.

Using the issues raised through the advice service, the charity continues to lobby and campaign for a better deal for older people.

www.counselandcare.org.uk

Acknowledgements

Thanks go to the compiler of this guide, Elizabeth McLennan, and the rest of the advice team at Counsel and Care, who provided invaluable guidance and assistance on the text.

Introduction

Getting started

Why does age take us by surprise? It seems to creep up on us all. Medical and technological developments in our modern society mean that everyone is now living longer, and we are enjoying more and more years in good health. On the whole, we like the benefits of a longer and healthier life – more time to spend with children and grandchildren, to travel, to develop our careers and to get our feet firmly on the property ladder.

However, this increased longevity has its downsides – there are ever increasing numbers of people with dementia (currently there are around 700,000 and this figure is expected to increase to 1.7 million in 2051, according to the Alzheimer's Society) and more older people are now living in residential care homes. The government's Social Exclusion Unit estimates that there are currently 1.2 million older people who are socially isolated, living alone, and who may have very little contact with their family or the rest of the outside world.

So, is there anything we can do to plan for old age, or to help our parents make arrangements for their retirement? What support is available from the state, what are our options and what information do we need? How much will it cost, and where can we go for help and guidance?

About this guide

This guide will provide you with all the answers to the above questions, as well as many other things you have probably never even considered. It will tell you what you can expect if you need to find care services or support for an older person and it will help you with the key points you need to know should you require information about your options in order to plan ahead or if you need to arrange care services urgently. This guide will give you a general knowledge about the social care system (what it is, who it supports), as well as information on how to put in place care services and who to contact. Also, it will provide details on how to complain if you have a problem, and how to plan in advance so that crisis situations can be avoided where possible. The guide contains many useful tips on what you should do to make sure that the care services you put in place are the best possible for your friend, neighbour or relative. It also gives you organisations to contact if you want more detailed information.

All of the information in this guide refers to England. Most of the legislation and practices are also relevant in Wales and Scotland. There are certain exceptions to this, which are noted specifically in the text. If you would like more information about the care and health system in Scotland, you can contact Age Concern Scotland (tel: 0845 125 9732; www.ageconcernscotland.org.uk). If you live in Wales, contact Age Concern Cymru (tel: 029 2043 1555; www.accymru.org.uk).

KEY FACTS AND FIGURES

During 2005–06:

- An estimated 1,200,000 people aged over 65 received social care services
- 491,000 received home care services
- 387,000 received equipment and adaptations
- 228,000 received professional support
- 136,000 received day care services

Source: The NHS Information Centre: Community Care Statistics 2005–06

So who is an 'older person'?

In today's terminology 'the elderly' are called 'older people'. When women turn 60, they are, by government definition, an 'older person'. For many years this has been 65 for men, and there are plans to increase this for women as well, so that by 2020 everyone over 65 will be an 'older person'. This means that they may become entitled to State Retirement Pension, Pension Guarantee Credit and other age-dependent benefits.

The challenges of older age

We know that as soon as people turn 60, they do not suddenly lose all their abilities, their financial management skills, and their desire to do new things and enjoy new experiences. However, cognitive and physical ability may start to decline gradually, and things which once were easy and straightforward become slightly more difficult, or may take more time. All of these can be managed with the right care and support, so that older people can continue to live independently for as long as they want.

Around one in five people over 80 experience symptoms of dementia, or Alzheimer's disease. This is a condition which affects the memory, and while in its milder forms people can carry on as before, when it is severe it is life limiting, and affects the way people live and what they can do on their own. Physical difficulties may also become more prevalent in older age due to illnesses such as arthritis, osteoporosis, Parkinson's disease, etc.

Older people are particularly vulnerable to financial difficulties, and, of course, these difficulties have more of an impact if the individual is unable to work. Pension problems have been widely recorded in the media in recent times, as some company schemes have collapsed and people's expectations on the state increased. Women who have taken time out of work to care for children or older relatives may not have built up enough National Insurance contributions to be eligible for the full State Retirement Pension.

The good news – services available

Most older people manage to live independently, without any support; for those who do need support and who may experience some of the difficulties described above, there is help at hand. With a little planning, many situations can be managed and coped with.

Benefits

Many older people become eligible for benefits, such as Attendance Allowance and Pension Guarantee Credit, which are available to those people who have physical or financial difficulties. There are many other benefits also available to older people which can help them maintain a comfortable standard of living in later life.

Social care

There is help available through your local social services department, which has a duty to provide services if an individual is in need of support, or at least provide information about how to arrange this type of care privately. Care packages can be arranged to provide support in someone's own home, or through a move into sheltered or extra care sheltered housing, or maybe a residential care home. There are many options available. Currently, social care is not free in England or Wales and is charged according to the income, capital and savings of the individual. In Scotland, social care services are provided free. These services can be provided either in a residential care home or in someone's own home.

Healthcare

People over 60 are the biggest users of the National Health Service in the UK. GPs are often the front line of enquiry for older people with a health difficulty, but there are many services available in hospitals and community health centres which are specifically targeted towards the needs of older people.

Information services and charities

There are many sources of information about all of the above, but often the problem is how to know where to look for them. However, there are some services, such as the Counsel and Care advice service (tel: 0845 300 7585; advice@counselandcare.org.uk), which provide tailored advice covering all of these areas. Many charities exist specifically to give guidance, support and help to people who are arranging care for a parent or older relative or friend. Their details can be found in the Appendix of this guide.

What is social care?

Social care is the name given to care provided to people in order that they can continue living in society. Social care can be provided informally, by friends and relatives, or it can be provided by the state, through social services departments in local councils. It is also available to buy privately, and there are charities and businesses which provide social care at a charge to the individual. Social care should be available to all people who are in need of support; for example, older people, young families, single mothers, those with learning disabilities, children, etc. It is different to healthcare, although the two are very closely related, and health and social care teams should be in communication with each other if they are both involved in providing care to an individual.

However, and this is a big however, recent times have seen the levels of support provided by social services subject to more stringent eligibility requirements, essentially to reduce the number of people who can claim support. It means that these days only those older people who have very high needs are supported by social services. While campaigning organisations, such as Counsel and Care, are working hard to change this so that more people can receive support, it is likely that if you or an older friend or relative have low level difficulties, such as being unable to go shopping or clean the house, then this support will need to be bought privately, or arranged within a circle of family and friends. This guide will show you how this can be put in place, and what needs to be considered for effective support services to be available to an older person and his carer.

CHAPTER 1

The types of care available

THIS CHAPTER COVERS THE FOLLOWING:

- When could someone need care?
- What care is available from social services and how is it provided?
- Contacting social services
- What services can be bought privately?
- Home care services
- Day centres
- Meals on wheels
- Respite care services
- Holidays for older people
- Telecare support
- Homeshare schemes
- Befriending services
- Transport and mobility support for older people
- Arranging for maintenance to a home
- Garden maintenance schemes
- Safety in the home
- Sheltered and extra care housing services
- Residential care homes

- Getting advice, information or advocacy
- Sources of further information about care and support

When could someone need care?

You are probably reading this guide if you are thinking about arranging care for an older relative, friend or neighbour. It may be that someone you know is finding it more difficult to get around, is struggling to lift heavy things in the home, or cannot cope with the weekly shopping and cleaning routine any more. If you are assisting a friend or relative (referred to as the 'older person' in this guide) to arrange help and support, or you are thinking about providing this yourself, read this chapter for a round-up of what help may be available, and where you should start looking. For many people, it is likely that with a combination of support from social services along with informal support, the older person will be able to remain living independently in his own home.

What care is available from social services and how is it provided?

Your first port of call is the social services department of the older person you are trying to find help for. This is a department of the local council where the older person lives, which provides services for individuals with care and support needs. It has to meet certain requirements for those who appear to need such care and support.

You can contact the social services department on behalf of the older person; he does not necessarily have to phone the department himself, although he does have to be aware of and willing to have the assessment. All social services departments can be contacted on the internet, and many now have online assessment tools which can make the process of assessment more streamlined. It may be easier to contact the department by telephone in the first instance, to establish whether it is able to support the older person. The duty social work team is the best place for initial contact.

Care provided by social services used to include a wide range of services, including home help, shopping and pension collecting, etc. However, in recent times, social services departments have become more financially careful, and so they can now only help those older people who have really acute needs, and who need quite intensive support.

If you know an older person who needs low levels of support with his daily living tasks, it is very unlikely that you will receive this service from your local social services department. Your options are to provide this support yourself, in an informal network of carers including other family and friends, or to arrange privately for a home care agency to visit him.

The more intensive type of support that social services may still be able to provide would cover things such as helping the older person out of bed in the morning and helping him to wash and dress, delivering and helping him to use incontinence pads, or it could be providing him with hot or microwaveable meals once a week. If the older person needs some nursing care as well, the social worker can arrange for all of the necessary assessments, so that he receives visits from a community nurse.

There is more information later on in this chapter about the particular types of care and support available, which may be an option for the older person.

Contacting social services

You should contact the older person's local social services department, even if you think that his needs are too low to be met by the services it provides. You will be able to find the department's telephone number in the older person's local telephone directory or library, or on the internet. You should ask to speak to the duty social worker and explain that you want to arrange an assessment of need for the older person. The social services department has a duty to arrange an assessment of need if the older person appears to be in need of services. You may find, though, that unless the needs of the older person are very severe, there will be a long wait for him to receive an assessment. Social workers often have high workloads, and the people with more severe needs are seen first.

What services can be bought privately?

All social care services can be bought privately, either through a home care agency or in a care home. The services can be arranged independently of the social services department in the older person's local council. However, it is always advisable to contact social services, even if you think that the older person may need to pay for care privately. Social services will be able to give advice on what the options are and it can provide information about what is available in the local area. It will also explain about funding options. While buying care privately is always an option, it must be carefully considered. What would happen to the older person if the source of funding ran out? How do you choose the best care service available? How can it be fully ensured that the care services are required, and are meeting the support needs of the older person? It may be that the older person is eligible for financial support towards the costs of his care, so it would be advisable to call and arrange to speak to a social worker about the situation before any services are put in place privately.

Home care services

For low level needs when an older person is living in his own home, the services of a home care agency may be suitable. An agency may provide:

- Carers to help people into and out of bed

- Help with washing and dressing

- Help with domestic cleaning and light household tasks

- Assistance with shopping, etc.

- Assistance with food preparation

Q What is a home care agency?

A A home care agency is an organisation which provides care assistants to older people in their own home. They are often run as businesses, so they charge a market rate for the services they provide, but some are operated by charitable or not-for-profit organisations. A home care agency can arrange for care assistants to visit people in their own home, but it is also able to assist with transport and meet other support needs. The hours and services are agreed between the agency and the older person and a contract is signed. Obviously, family can be involved in arranging this contract, if the older person wishes. The older person would complete a time sheet which is then passed to the agency showing what services have been provided in an individual week, and this is used to invoice for the services provided.

Services from a home care agency can be arranged by contacting individual providers directly. It may be that there are a number of services available in your local area (look in your local telephone directory), but if you want to research further or find out more, contact the United Kingdom Home Care Agency (tel: 020 8288 1551; www.ukhca.co.uk) or the Commission for Social Care Inspection (CSCI) (tel: 0845 015 0120; www.csci.org.uk), which both carry lists of registered agencies. CSCI is the body which inspects and regulates all home care agencies and care homes in England. In Scotland, this body is the Scottish Commission for the Regulation of Care, and in Wales it is the Care Standards Inspectorate for Wales. All three organisations carry details of all of the registered services available in their area, together with inspection reports. Do try to speak to other family and friends who live in the same area as the older person to see if they have had experience of a particular home care agency. Can they recommend one? Personal stories of local agencies can be just as reliable as inspection reports and regulatory bodies.

As emphasised above, it is important to contact the social services department first, before arranging any home care services on a private basis. As well as carrying out an assessment of need, the department will be able to provide advice about funding care, as well as give you a list of its approved providers. These are the organisations which it uses locally to provide services for people who need support.

While there are advantages in buying care privately (you are not restricted by social services and its eligibility criteria), the disadvantage is that the older person may be restricted by his available budget. Buying services privately is very expensive and home care may cost up to £16–18 per hour (but this figure does vary according to the area you live in). It is worth considering whether the older person can afford these fees on an ongoing basis, and whether his family is able to assist with financial support. Also, do consider which benefits the older person is receiving as, in many cases, older people are eligible for benefits which remain unclaimed. Additional benefits are available for people who have limited mobility, care and support needs, and who are over a certain age and are on a low income. Increasing an older person's income through benefits means that he is more likely to be able to afford support services and there are more options available to him. See Chapter 8 of this guide for more information about benefits and how to help someone claim them.

Day centres

If the older person is still living in his own home, it may be worth considering a day centre for a few days a week. These are centres which provide company and activities, a meal, and some help with personal care. Some day centres provide support for people who have a particular disability or illness; for example, Parkinson's disease or Alzheimer's disease. They are generally provided by local councils and so the older person would need to be assessed by social services, as outlined earlier in this chapter. Day centre support can be very useful, as it can help to maintain someone's independence and it can teach new skills and provide mental stimulation. It can also provide a useful break for the carer of an older person.

If you think that this would be a useful option for the older person, you can go along and visit the premises, to meet the staff and the manager and the older people who already use the centre.

In many areas additional day centres are now provided by private care homes or voluntary organisations, such as Age Concern (tel: 0845 600 2001; www.ageconcern.org.uk) and the Alzheimer's Society (tel: 0845 300 0336; www.alzheimers.org.uk).

Meals on wheels

The council's social services can provide meals for older people who have difficulty shopping or preparing hot meals for themselves. The meals will usually be delivered on a weekly basis as frozen portions to be heated up in an oven or microwave. This service may be arranged by the council's social services but provided by local private or voluntary agencies, such as the Women's Royal Voluntary Service (WRVS). There is usually a charge for each meal. If you think that this service would be beneficial for the older person, contact the social services department in his local council.

Respite care services

Respite care can be provided so that a carer can have a break from his caring responsibilities. In exceptional cases it can mean a care worker 'living-in' with the cared-for person while the carer goes away, but it will usually involve the cared-for person staying in a care home temporarily while the carer has a complete break. This can be arranged in a 'rolling' programme; for example, every six weeks. It is important to get the period between each break arranged so that it does not affect the cared-for person's Attendance Allowance (AA) or Disability Living Allowance (DLA). (More details about benefits can be found in Chapter 8 of this guide.) Some voluntary agencies can provide care workers to sit in while the carer goes out to work or for a social activity. Respite care can be arranged through the social services department or through the GP or hospital consultant if the older person has medical needs, but it depends on the local arrangements available.

Holidays for older people

Social services departments are required to assist with holidays for people with disabilities in accordance with the Chronically Sick and Disabled Persons Act 1973. Assistance may mean as little as arranging transport to or from the holiday and often does not mean any funding to pay for the holiday. However, if you think that the older person would benefit from a break, it is worth considering. There are charities who will also consider paying for, or contributing towards, a holiday for an older person. The charity may contribute to a particular portion of the costs of the holiday, and it may expect the older person to contribute a proportion of the costs himself. For more details about financial support from charities, see Chapter 9 of this guide.

Telecare support

Many councils can now provide telecare services to assist older people who live in their own home. Telecare is technology which can help monitor an older person's safety and well-being if he is at risk of harming himself or someone else. Examples of telecare services are bed sensors to see if someone gets out of bed in the night but does not return, alarms which can signal if the gas or a water tap has been left on, and devices to alert the resident to the fact that the front door may have been left ajar accidentally. Telecare can also help people who may lack mental capacity, or who are developing early symptoms of dementia and who may be forgetful.

If the older person has an assessment from social services, it may be that he receives some sort of telecare support within his care package. Smaller telecare devices are available to buy and, in some cases, are quite affordable. You can contact the Disabled Living Foundation (tel: 0845 130 9177; www.dlf.org.uk) for more information about what is available.

Homeshare schemes

Homeshare is a scheme which has been established for people who are having difficulty living on their own in their home, and who need a bit of extra help with tasks and chores. Homeshare will match an older person with someone younger, providing the older person with help and reassurance, and the younger person with accommodation. People are very carefully matched to ensure that they will be compatible. Such schemes are not available in every area, but more information can be obtained from the organising charity Homeshare (tel: 020 7351 3851; www.homeshare.org).

Befriending services

These are services run by local voluntary organisations which can provide volunteers to help older people make friends and feel less socially isolated. A 'befriender' may visit once a week for a cup of tea and a chat, or may be able to take the older person out for the day. If you think that the older person may benefit from this type of service, you can find one by contacting your local Age Concern. Details of the different Age Concerns in England, Wales and Scotland can be found in the Appendix.

Transport and mobility support for older people

Often people become socially isolated because they have difficulties with their mobility. If the older person has a disability or walking problem, he may wish to be assessed by an occupational therapist or physiotherapist to see what exercises or equipment may help him to mobilise more safely. If he is unable to mobilise safely out-of-doors, then he may be entitled to a wheelchair (his GP should be contacted if it is felt that a wheelchair is needed). Alternatively, a motorised scooter can provide him with an independent means to get out and about. (If he was on the higher rate mobility component of Disability Living Allowance before he was 65, he may be eligible to hire purchase a motorised scooter under the Motability scheme. For more information about this, contact the Disabled Living Foundation (tel: 0845 130 9177; www.dlf.org.uk).)

Some equipment, such as a motorised scooter, is not available from the council's social services, but if you cannot afford the purchase price, it is possible to borrow the equipment or raise the money through charities. Shopmobility is a national charity that hires out scooters to disabled people to enable them to shop and to visit leisure and commercial facilities in the local area. Each local area has a slightly different scheme, and different charges. For your local Shopmobility scheme, contact the head office on 0845 644 2446. Shopmobility offers training so that older people can use the scooters they hire and they often have volunteer escorts that can be booked when a scooter is hired.

Transport and getting out and about

If the older person is having trouble getting around safely when he is outside his home, you can help him to locate his nearest sources of support. Most local areas have a community transport scheme, such as Dial-a-Ride, which provides door-to-door transport for older and disabled people. To arrange these services, the older person would need to have an assessment from the social services department. In some areas there are volunteer schemes which arrange lifts for people who have difficulty leaving the house without support. You can contact your local Age Concern or Women's Royal Voluntary Service (tel: 01235 442 900; www.wrvs.org.uk) for details of any local schemes.

Some councils offer local people with a mobility impairment reduced fares in taxis. This can be known as a 'concessions fare', taxi voucher or taxicard scheme. The social services department will have the details of this scheme if it operates in your local area.

Arranging for maintenance to a home

It may be that the older person lives in his own home still, and that there are maintenance tasks which need to be arranged so that he can live safely and keep everything in good working order.

If the older person owns his own home or is a private tenant, he can receive information and advice from his local Home Improvement Agency (HIA). These not-for-profit schemes specialise in providing advice and support on issues of maintenance and adaptation to the homes of older and disabled people. To find out if there is one in his local area, contact Foundations (tel: 01457 891 909; www.foundations.uk.com), which keeps a database of Home Improvement Agencies across the country. If the older person is a private tenant, he will need the permission of the landlord before he undertakes any major alterations or repairs.

If the older person is a council or housing association tenant, he should ring his landlord in the first instance, explaining what repairs need to be undertaken. If the work remains uncompleted, write to the landlord formally, asking for a response in writing. The council or housing association must inspect the proposed repairs and arrange for them to be undertaken.

Garden maintenance schemes

If the older person is having trouble maintaining his garden, there may be local organisations which can provide volunteers to help. Help the Aged runs a gardening programme which helps local organisations to develop gardening assistance schemes for older people. His local Age Concern will also know of any schemes which operate locally. It may also be worth contacting the local volunteer bureau to see if it has any volunteers who can help. Contact Volunteering England (tel: 0845 305 6979; www.volunteering.org.uk) for more details of your local volunteer bureau. If you live in Wales, contact Volunteering Wales (www.volunteering-wales.net). If you live in Scotland, contact Volunteer Development Scotland (www.vds.org.uk).

Safety in the home

Sometimes older people who live alone do not feel safe or may feel vulnerable, but there are measures which can be taken to reduce the fear of danger or harm.

- **Community alarms:** If the older person cannot get out or he lives alone, it can be reassuring and essential to know that he is able to contact someone in an emergency. There are many types of community alarms available for older people. Normally they are worn as badges, wrist bands or pendants and if they are pressed, an alarm is raised at a call centre. Someone from the centre will call back to find out the nature of the problem. The staff can speak to the older person via the alarm unit so that if the older person is unable to get to the telephone, he can still be contacted. After the member of staff has spoken to the older person, or if the person does not reply, he will arrange suitable help by contacting the nominated key holder (usually a family member) or by calling the emergency services. The cost of these systems varies. Some are provided by local council housing departments or social services departments, and others will be provided by a voluntary group.

- **Security:** The crime prevention officer at the local police station will be able to give advice about the security of someone's home. In some areas, he can put people in touch with local schemes which provide low cost security improvements, such as window locks, door locks and spyholes. Help the Aged runs a national scheme for people over 60 on a low income called 'HandyVan', which can install equipment such as door chains, spyholes, window locks, etc. You can contact the organisation on 01255 372 999. It is important that the older person takes precautions to prevent his being a victim of crime; for example, he should not let anyone into his home without being sure about the caller's identification and/or without a pre-arranged appointment. Many council services and electricity and gas companies have a special safety scheme which older people can join. The older person will need to contact his utility providers to see what scheme they operate.

- **Safety of appliances:** There is a risk of people being killed and injured because of dangerous gas and electricity appliances. It is important that all appliances are checked regularly to ensure that they are not faulty or leaking. You can speak to the gas and electricity suppliers of the older person for more information as they may provide free safety schemes for older people and those with disabilities. If a gas or electric appliance is condemned and the older person has no heating or cooking facilities because of this, you should contact his local council's social services department immediately as it has a duty of care to vulnerable people. The department should advise you of emergency support that can be provided until a replacement appliance can be purchased.

- **Fire safety:** It is important to have smoke detectors fitted in someone's home. You could also consider having carbon monoxide detectors in the property. There are specially adapted fire detectors for deaf people. If you want to explore the option of fitting one for the older person, you can obtain more information from your local fire station or the Disabled Living Foundation (tel: 0845 130 9177; www. dlf.org.uk).

Sheltered and extra care housing services

Sheltered housing and extra care housing services are accommodation options for older people but they are not well known, despite 500,000 people living in such schemes in the UK. Most local councils have sheltered housing schemes available for older people and there are a number of private providers across the UK which provide similar services on a private basis.

Sheltered housing is a form of independent living where the older person rents accommodation in a scheme of around 10–20 similar properties. Each has its own front door, and all of the domestic facilities you would expect. Accommodation is generally unfurnished, so carpets, washing machines, etc. need to be supplied by the individual. The benefit of living in a sheltered housing scheme is that there is support available on site, should it be necessary. For instance, nearly every scheme will have a call alarm system, which means that if the older person has a fall, he can call for assistance. There are also scheme managers available who can arrange to visit or call once a day to make sure that the older person is all right. Best of all, the older person is able to retain the independence he is used to, but with the security of knowing help is available if he needs it.

Extra care housing works on a similar principle to sheltered housing. The older person has a property to himself, which has its own front door, kitchen, bathroom, living area, etc. The difference in an extra care scheme is that it caters for people who need more intensive support; for example, a visit from a carer to assist the older person with some of his personal care needs, helping him to be washed and dressed in the morning, or helping him to bed at night. The carers will visit, but then leave again, so that for most of the day the older person is able to live independently as he would normally do if he lived at home.

You can find details of available sheltered and extra care housing schemes in a local area by contacting the Elderly Accommodation Counsel (tel: 020 7820 1343; www.housingcare.org).

Residential care homes

It may be that the needs of the older person cannot be met by the type of service provided by a home care agency, and are also too intensive to be met successfully in a sheltered or extra care housing scheme, and so in this situation residential care may be needed. Again, this can be arranged privately or by contacting social services. As with home care services, it is always advisable to contact your social services department, even if it is likely that the care will be funded privately, because the department will be able to offer guidance and information about the options available. It may be that the older person is eligible for financial support towards the care home fees, and it is always a good idea to obtain an assessment of need, so that you know what you are looking for in a care home.

If you are in the position of needing to find care for the older person, it can be a stressful time. However, it is important, where possible, to maintain good communication with him, and to involve him in as many decisions as possible about where care and support should be received and what services are arranged. It can be very easy to get swept along in arranging the services without properly asking his opinion or thoughts about what you are putting in place. If you are working with other siblings to arrange the support, it may be worth sitting down as a family to discuss what is being arranged, to make sure that everyone is happy.

> **Q** How can I get details of care homes in the area where the older person lives?
>
> **A** To find out about the care homes in his local area, contact the Elderly Accommodation Counsel (tel: 020 7820 1343; www. housingcare.org), which holds a national database of all care homes, and which can advise which homes may be suitable. Alternatively, you can contact the Commission for Social Care Inspection (tel: 0845 120 7111; www.csci.org.uk). This organisation will also have details of the types of home available, together with the sort of needs it can meet. The social services department in his local council should also have a list of approved providers which it currently uses to provide services.

Residential care can be expensive, averaging around £400 per week. Nursing care homes are around £600 per week and dementia care homes up to £800 per week. These figures are likely to be even higher in the South East of England. The average length of stay in a care home is about two years, so make sure that if the older person is paying privately, consideration has been given to what you would do if the money ran out, or if you think more support may be needed in the future.

There is more detailed information on how home care services and residential care homes are funded in Chapters 2 and 4 of this guide. There are also further details about exactly what support you can expect from social services, as well as what to think about if you or the older person are paying privately for the services. Be sure to read these chapters thoroughly before making any arrangements.

Getting advice, information or advocacy

Knowing that an older person has a need for care is one thing, but arranging it can be really difficult, especially if this has to be fitted around other existing responsibilities for children, or your job. This is why it is crucial that you make sure that you receive good information and advice so that you make the best use of your time, and avoid any crisis situations. If you obtain advice at the beginning of the process, you can then make sure that you are asking the right questions and getting everything that the older person is entitled to. There are many advice services available, both in your local area and nationally. Your local social services department will hold details of local advice organisations and support groups which will provide information.

Independent advocacy is also important in situations where there is the potential that the older person may not feel able to speak out about what care and support he needs or would like to receive. Often it is helpful to arrange for the services of an advocate when there are a number of professionals or family members involved in a situation, particularly where there are differing views.

An independent advocate is a person who represents the views and wishes of the older person. He will meet with the older person to establish what he feels about a situation, to see if he has any questions or concerns which have not been addressed, and to put forward these opinions on behalf of the older person. An independent advocate is someone who is not connected to the organisations involved in providing care for the older person; for instance, the hospital, or the social services department. It is important that the advocate is non-biased so that he is only influenced by the older person.

Independent advocacy can also work when the older person may lack mental capacity, and the advocate can even be crucial in situations where there is a dispute about the older person's care where there may be an assumption that he is unable to express an opinion. Some advocates are trained to communicate and work specifically with people who have dementia. It should be assumed that an individual may have the capacity to make decisions, and could have the capacity to make one decision, but not another; for example, to communicate what he would like to wear that day, but not what he would like to eat for lunch. A psychiatrist or psychogeriatrician will be able to establish whether the individual is able to make a particular decision, and the advocate will represent the views and best wishes of the older person, as far as possible.

The Mental Capacity Act 2005 has set out formally people's entitlements to receive advocacy services. In situations where an older person lacks mental capacity, has no family or friends able to represent him, and who needs to make a decision about his accommodation or a serious medical treatment, he can access the services of an Independent Mental Capacity Advocate (IMCA). The professionals involved in the care of the older person should involve an IMCA to establish as far as possible what his wishes are.

A local advocacy service can be found by contacting Advocacy Resource Exchange (tel: 0845 122 8633; www.advocacyresource.net).

Sources of further information about care and support

There are a number of advice agencies available which can help with your search for information about the support available to older people. Their contact details can be found in the Appendix.

Age Concern has a large range of information available, including an enquiry line and a range of fact sheets. It also operates smaller local agencies around England, Scotland and Wales, which can provide help with benefits, finding a care home in the local area, and a range of home care and community services.

The **Citizens Advice Bureau** can provide advice on a wide range of issues, including benefits and debt law. There are local branches which provide advice and support for people who live within their particular local area. (www.adviceguide.org.uk can provide the contact telephone numbers of local branches.)

The **Commission for Social Care Inspection** (for England, or the Scottish Commission for the Regulation of Care for Scotland, or the Care Standards Inspectorate for Wales) is responsible for regulating and inspecting care services provided by care homes. It carries information about what registered services are available in your local area, along with recent inspection reports.

Counsel and Care is a national advice service which can offer information and help about any issues affecting people over 60, along with their families and carers. A comprehensive range of fact sheets is available to download from its website.

Elderly Accommodation Counsel can give information about local sheltered and extra care housing schemes, along with residential, nursing and dementia care homes. It has details of local vacancies and the services offered in individual homes.

Help the Aged has a comprehensive range of information about all issues affecting people over 60, from both the website and its information line, called Seniorline.

United Kingdom Home Care Association represents home care agencies, and can provide information about what is available in a local area.

CHAPTER 2

How to pay for home care services

THIS CHAPTER COVERS THE FOLLOWING:

- Setting up home care services
- Having an assessment of need
- After an assessment has taken place
- What sorts of services are available from the council?
- The importance of the care plan
- Changes to services received from the social services department
- Requesting a review of care needs
- Refusing services and other problems
- The social services financial assessment
- How much is the council allowed to charge for its services?
- What are direct payments and how can they help the older person?
- Paying privately for home care

So, it may be that the older person is living by himself or with a partner in his own home, but he is beginning to struggle with some daily living tasks. You and the older person have decided that home care services are the best way forward for him. Home care services will provide that little bit of extra help, to help keep the older person active and independent for as long as possible. But what happens next? This chapter outlines the various care services available.

Setting up home care services

Before you do anything else, contact the social services department at the local council where the older person lives. Contact details will be in your local telephone directory or your library. You should ask to speak to a duty social worker in the older people's team, explaining the circumstances of the enquiry. You can phone on behalf of the older person, and just explain that you are doing so. The social worker will probably want to speak to the older person himself at some point, but for routine enquiries, a third party enquiry is fine.

The social worker who you speak to may want to know brief details of the difficulties the older person is experiencing, so you should have these details to hand. If it appears to the social worker that the older person may need assistance, he should carry out an assessment of the older person's needs, regardless of his financial circumstances.

If it appears to the social worker that there is no urgent need for an assessment, there may be a wait for a visit. There are no time limits which define how quickly an older person should be assessed, although if urgent assistance is needed, the council's social services should assess quickly, and the department is likely to have its own internal timescales. If you think that the older person needs this urgent support, you should make this clear over the telephone and ask for an immediate assessment. If there are any delays in assessment, you can ask to see a copy of the timescales, which may have been set by the social services department, and you can complain on behalf of the older person if you have continued difficulties. You can find out more about making a complaint about services in Chapter 10 of this guide.

Having an assessment of need

An assessment of need will be carried out by a social worker or care manager to establish what the actual care needs of the older person are. He will ask a series of questions about the daily life of the older person, to see where he may need support. If you want to be present at the assessment of the older person, this is fine, as it may be helpful if it is likely that he will forget key details, or he just needs some moral support. If it is helpful, a GP, nurse or other professional can also request for an assessment of need to be carried out.

It is a 'duty' on the social services department to carry out an assessment of need if it appears that someone is in need of services. In reality, this means that if the older person is struggling with any aspect of his daily life, he should be eligible to receive an assessment. If he is refused an assessment, it may be because the social worker you spoke to was not completely clear about the difficulties that the older person is experiencing. If this happens, it may be helpful to write a letter to the social services department, fully outlining the needs of the older person and explaining the needed services in more detail. It may also be useful to obtain a copy of the criteria that the social services department uses when it is considering people for assessment. The criteria should be published, and made available to people who request it.

Assessments should be conducted under what is called the 'Single Assessment Process', or SAP. This is where professionals from health and social care, and other agencies if they are involved, conduct just one assessment of someone's needs. The assessment should look at all aspects of the older person's situation, and should take account of health needs, social care needs, etc. It is designed so that the older person does not have to have multiple assessments where they repeat the same information each time. The social services department should ensure that the assessment is carried out by skilled and competent staff and that contributions from more qualified and specialist professionals are available if a more detailed assessment is required.

The type of assessment received by the older person will depend on the difficulties that he is experiencing. For example, if the person is having difficulty preparing a hot meal, he may be assessed by a simple interview and then provided with meals on wheels as a service. If the older person has more complex difficulties, he will need a more detailed assessment, sometimes known as a 'comprehensive assessment'. A social worker, or care manager, will usually co-ordinate this, although with many social services and health bodies it may be another designated assessor. He may also contact other people involved in the individual's care, such as a care worker, district nurse, GP or medical specialist. Occupational therapists and physiotherapists are also often involved to ensure that the older person remains as independent as possible with recommended aids, adaptations or exercises; this is called a 'multi-disciplinary assessment'.

An assessment will usually be carried out in someone's home, normally by social services staff; for example, a social worker or care manager. Whether or not you are at the assessment of the older person, it may be helpful to help him make a list of the difficulties he has been experiencing, so that they are all considered in the assessment.

It is very important that within the detailed Single Assessment Process, the individual areas of someone's life are taken into consideration. This includes the assessment of not only health and welfare needs, but also emotional, psychological and religious needs. In the Single Assessment Process, these are known as 'domains'. The following issues should always be considered in a comprehensive assessment:

The older person's point of view

- Problems and issues in his own words
- His expectations and motivation

Clinical background

- Any medical problems he has currently or in the past
- Whether he has had any falls
- Any medication he takes

Disease prevention

- His blood pressure
- His weight and nutrition
- The vaccinations he has had
- Whether he drinks or smokes
- Whether he takes regular exercise
- Whether the older person has had regular cervical and breast screens

Personal care and physical well-being

- Whether he can look after himself
- Whether he has any problems with his teeth and gums
- Whether he has any problems with his feet
- Whether he has any pressure sores or skin breakdown
- Any difficulties with mobility
- Any problems with continence

Senses

- Whether any sight or hearing problems cause difficulties

Mental health

- Any mental health difficulties (such as dementia or depression)
- Problems with his memory

Relationships

- The relationships he has, and wishes to maintain
- The friends or people he sees socially
- The relationship he has with any carer, or someone who looks after him

Safety

- Whether he has been abused or suffered from neglect
- Any other problems with personal safety
- Whether he is a threat to other people's safety

Immediate environment and resources

- Whether he is able to look after his home
- Whether his accommodation is suitable
- Whether he needs advice about his finances or welfare benefits
- Whether he can get to the shops and other facilities and services

Lifestyle choices

- Where he wants to live

- His wish to maintain hobbies and interests

If you have concerns that these issues have not been covered adequately in the assessment that the older person receives, you can raise it at the time, during the assessment, or you can contact the social worker who carried out the assessment and ask him to consider the aspects which were not covered. It is important that all aspects are considered during an assessment, because otherwise there is a danger that some needs are given more importance than others.

After an assessment has taken place

After the assessment has taken place, the results will be set against the council's eligibility criteria for services. The eligibility criteria describe the type of needs that the council services will meet. All councils use the same guidelines for their criteria, which are published for national use by the Department of Health, but individual councils are allowed to choose what level of need they will meet.

The criteria outline four levels of care need:

1. **Critical:** When life is threatened or significant health problems have developed or will develop.

2. **Substantial:** Where there is an inability to carry out the majority of personal care or domestic routines.

3. **Moderate:** Where there is an inability to carry out several personal care routines.

4. **Low:** Where there is an inability to carry out one or two personal care routines.

The criteria also cover other aspects of care and welfare, but these are general examples of the level of needs they refer to.

At the moment, two-thirds of local councils only provide services to those people whose needs are assessed as being substantial or critical. This means that many older people are not eligible for services if their needs are relatively low.

If the older person is assessed as having needs but they are too low for the local council to meet, he should still be provided with a written statement of his needs. This is useful if the older person decides to buy support services privately from a home care agency, because the agency may not need to reassess the needs of the older person if it can see a copy of this document. If the council does not provide the support services to the older person, the social worker should make sure that the older person is able to arrange that support himself, or that he knows what options are open to him. The social services department should also record the outcome of the assessment as being an 'unmet need', so that it can keep track of the support that it is not able to provide and it should help the department to plan services in the future.

> **Q** Why do eligibility criteria vary from area to area?
>
> **A** Local councils can set their own eligibility criteria for social care services. They do, however, have to base their criteria on central government guidance, called 'Fair Access to Care Services'. It means that they are allowed to set particular levels of need which they will meet.

What sorts of services are available from the council?

Aids and adaptations: These are items which can assist around the home; for example, a seat fitted in the shower to reduce the risk of slipping, handrails in the bathroom and up the stairs, wheelchair ramps, gadgets for the kitchen, etc. These are available from the social services department following an assessment from a social worker or an occupational therapist. If they cost under £1,000, they should be provided free of charge. Many of these aids are available to buy very cheaply, and are available from Disabled Living Foundation outlets (tel: 0845 130 9177; www.dlf.org.uk). Because there can often be a wait for an assessment from social services, if the item that the older person needs is quite cheap and can be easily installed, you could consider buying and arranging for it to be fitted yourself.

Home carers (care assistants): These are support staff who help with washing, dressing, meals, cleaning, household tasks, shopping and the withdrawal of pensions.

Transport: Many social services departments can organise community transport services, such as Dial-a-Ride, which is specifically for disabled and older people to use when public transport may not be convenient. Dial-a-Ride will pick up and drop off the older person at selected times and will take him directly to his destination. There is a small charge and the transport needs to be booked in advance. Some councils use volunteer drivers and carers. People over 60 are also eligible for free off-peak local bus travel. You can help the older person apply for a bus pass, and the form can be obtained in local Post Offices.

Day centres: These can provide company and social activities, a meal and some help with personal care. Transport is usually provided for collecting the older person and taking him back home again. Some day centres can assist with bathing.

Meals on wheels: These are hot meal services which are provided to people who may have difficulty cooking safely. Meals are delivered daily or weekly, depending on how vulnerable the older person is, and are heated up in the microwave or oven.

Telecare: These are aids and adaptations which rely on sensors or monitors to help an older person stay safe in his own home. For example, beds can be fitted with devices which can tell when someone has got out of bed in the night. If he does not get back into bed again within a certain time, a call centre is alerted in case the older person has fallen over and was unable to get back into bed.

All of the above services from the council will be provided after the older person has received a financial assessment. This will take into account his income and what he owns in savings and property, before making charges for services. This is covered in more detail later in this chapter.

CASE STUDY

Mrs Stewart is 77 and has had a severe stroke which has left her immobile and severely disabled. She receives at least two hours' help at home each day. She has help to get out of bed, wash, dress and prepare her breakfast. A second carer does her shopping and housework. Another carer returns in the evening to help her to go to bed and provides her tea. Mrs Stewart has a hot meal provided five days a week at lunchtimes by the council meals on wheels service and a neighbour provides her weekend meals.

The importance of the care plan

Once an assessment has taken place, and it has been agreed that the older person will be provided with services by the local council, he should receive a written care plan. This should clearly outline his individual needs, including his emotional, psychological, cultural, social and spiritual needs. The care plan should also include details of how the person will receive the support he needs. If services are being provided, the care plan should detail who will be providing the service, along with details of who to contact if there are any problems.

Care plans should be agreed between the older person and the social worker and should include any concerns which have been raised. Both the older person and any interested relatives can discuss with the social worker if it is felt that an amendment may be needed, or if a certain issue has not been addressed. Both the service user and the social worker should sign and date the care plan, and both should keep a copy of the final document.

Changes to services received from the social services department

Once the care plan has been agreed, and both parties have signed the document, the social services department is not able to withdraw or change the services provided, unless it reassesses the older person's care needs. If changes to services are proposed, you should make sure that the older person has received another assessment, and you should request one if none has been arranged. If services are withdrawn or changed without an assessment, you should consider making a complaint on behalf of the older person.

Requesting a review of care needs

If the needs of the older person change, or it is not felt that the assessment took all of his care needs into account, it is possible to request a review of the assessment. If you are arranging this on behalf of the older person, you should try to contact the person who originally carried out the assessment, or you can contact the duty social work desk. Regular reviews of the older person's care needs should also be carried out, at least once every year, and should involve other related professionals and any family or friends involved in the care of the older person.

Refusing services and other problems

Government guidance advises local council social services that it must meet an older person's assessed needs if he falls within the eligibility criteria, but it may consider its budget when deciding how to meet these needs. This means that the department may offer an individual his 'preferred option', which may be the cheapest option. For example, if 24-hour care is needed, the council's social services may decide that the older person's needs can be met most economically in a residential care home rather than by arranging for services in his own home.

The common example of this happening occurs when an older person is living in his own home, and he needs intensive home care services in order to live safely. The social services department may decide in this case that it is cheaper for it to provide care in a residential care home, rather than provide four visits a day from a home care worker. The department is within its rights to do this, as it will still be meeting the assessed needs of the older person.

However, social services cannot force someone to go into a care home, unless there are specific mental health reasons when it may be necessary. If the older person insists on staying in his own home in these circumstances, he may not receive all of the help that he requires. You can assist him by encouraging him to request a review of the original assessment of the care needs and argue that he needs to remain in his own home. (This is when emotional and psychological needs become especially important.) If the social services will not increase the level of the care at home, the older person may have to sign an agreement to acknowledge that some of his needs are not being met. The social services should not refuse to provide any services at all, but it may be necessary to negotiate with the department to agree that unpaid carers will meet some of the care needs or that additional private care will be paid for by the older person.

If it is felt at any time that the older person is being pressurised to move into a care home against his will, you may wish to seek further advice about his rights from an advice agency, such as Counsel and Care (tel: 0845 300 7585; www.counselandcare.org.uk).

It may be that the older person is offered services that he does not want; for example, he may not want to go to a day centre or have care staff visiting him at home. If this is the case, you should discuss any concerns with his social worker or care manager and try to arrange for the care needs to be reassessed and the services changed. The older person has the right to refuse services, and the social services department cannot force anyone to receive help.

The social services financial assessment

If the older person is assessed as needing services, and the council has agreed that it can meet these needs and provide the services, the older person will have a financial assessment which is also carried out by social services. This is because services from a local council are not free and, depending on resources, the older person may be asked to pay all or part of the cost of the service. In Scotland any services which are arranged by the local council and which provide personal care are free of charge. This is because in Scotland personal care is paid for by the Scottish Executive. Other types of support are charged for in Scotland; for instance, help with domestic tasks from a carer. In England and Wales all services, including care services, are subject to a charge by the local council.

In England, Wales and Scotland the local council will conduct a financial assessment which looks at the amount of money the older person has in savings, as well as his income from pensions and benefits. If the older person has joint savings with his partner or spouse, half of this amount will be taken into account. The income of a spouse or partner should not be taken into account in a financial assessment, although some councils do ask for this information. There is, however, no obligation to share information about a spouse or partner's income when an assessment is carried out.

Q Is the value of a house taken into account in charging for home care services?

A No, the older person's home should not be taken into account. If it is, you should question this with the person carrying out the assessment. If necessary, you should raise your concerns with the person making the assessment and if it remains unresolved, consider making a formal complaint. See Chapter 10 of this guide if you feel that a complaint is necessary.

How much is the council allowed to charge for its services?

In the same way that councils can set eligibility criteria for services, they can also set their own charging policies. However, this must be in accordance with the guidance set out by central government. Any charge that is made for services must be 'reasonable' according to this guidance, called 'Fairer Charging Policies for Home Care and Other Non-Residential Care Services'. The charge should not take the older person below the level of Pension Guarantee Credit (the level of weekly income the government sets for people over 60 to live on), which in 2007–08 is £119.05, plus a 25 per cent buffer. So, in reality, the older person should be left with at least £148.81 per week after the charges for services. If someone is being charged so much that he has less than this to live on each week, a formal complaint should be raised. Please see Chapter 10 for further details about raising a complaint.

If the older person has difficulty meeting the charges he receives for services, he can request that the social services department consider a reduction in its charges. The services cannot be withdrawn if the charges are not paid by the older person, but the department is within its rights to pursue the debt, if the charges are considered to be 'reasonable'.

The social services department should publish information on its charging policy and how it calculates how much an individual is expected to pay.

You should consider whether the older person is receiving all of the benefits that he is entitled to, such as Attendance Allowance or Disability Living Allowance, which can help him pay for support services. For more information about the benefits available to older people, please see Chapter 8 of this guide.

Q Why do charges for services vary from area to area?

A In the same way that councils set eligibility criteria, they are also allowed to set their own individual charging policies. Again, these policies should be based on guidance from central government called *'Fairer Charging'*. Because of this, one council may have a very different charging policy from another, and they often have different budgets for social care services. For example, some local councils do not charge at all for home care services, but it is more common for services to be charged per hour. This can range from £4.50 to £18 per hour, and some services are charged per item, such as meals on wheels or community transport.

What are direct payments and how can they help the older person?

If the older person is assessed by the council as needing home care services, as well as being told what the council can provide, he should be given the option of direct payments instead of these services. Direct payments are essentially cash payments given to the individual, instead of services. This means that the older person is able to 'employ' a care assistant to provide the support he needs, and he organises this himself, or with help from a relative or friend. It is possible to have a combination of some home care services provided directly by the council and others arranged by the individual.

The principle behind direct payments is that the older person is able to retain more control and choice over the services he receives. In practice, older people have found them really useful and they can be used for a wide range of services, not just home care. For example, some people have used their direct payment to employ a gardener to help keep their garden tidy, or they have employed someone to take them out in a car for a ride once a week.

Do not be put off by the apparent complexity of the direct payments scheme – in practice it is much easier, and much more flexible, than it can first appear. If you think that the older person may choose this option, it is possible for a friend or relative to help him manage his money, so if you are looking for care services on behalf of someone else, you could help him manage this. One restriction for direct payments is that the money cannot be used to pay a relative to provide care, but it could be given to a next door neighbour for his help, for example. There are also many local Independent Living Groups that can help manage the processes involved in the direct payments scheme. You can find the Independent Living Group which is local to the older person by contacting the Independent Living Association (www.independentliving.co.uk).

CASE STUDY

Mrs Smith is 81 and lives on her own in her own home. She has a number of close friends from her local church who visit every now and again to take her to the shops for heavy items, but she is beginning to struggle with daily tasks because her arthritis makes it very painful to walk. She is also beginning to lose her sight, and some household tasks are quite dangerous for her to do on her own. Mrs Smith receives an assessment of need from her local social services department, and is found to be eligible for services.

She is adamant that she does not want anyone she does not know coming into her house, as she is wary of strangers, and so she decides instead to take her support in the form of a direct payment. Every week she receives £50 which she can use however she wants, provided she is able to account for how it has been spent. Mrs Smith decides that she will employ the niece of one of her friends to visit her during the day two times a week. She will help her prepare meals which can be frozen and reheated later in the week, as well as help her with simple household tasks, such as washing clothes, ironing and cleaning. This arrangement suits them both – Mrs Smith is able to have her needs met in exactly the way she wants, at times which suit her, and by someone that she knows and trusts. The young carer is also happy as her job fits around the times that she has to be in university for lectures.

Paying privately for home care

If the older person has received an assessment from social services and is found not to be eligible, it is likely that his needs are not thought to be high enough to meet the criteria. In this situation, the care will need to be provided either by informal networks of family or friends, or by finding a home care agency and employing it directly to undertake the caring tasks required.

If the older person needs to pay privately for his care services, you can help make sure that he is receiving all of the benefits he is eligible for. This is very important, as buying home care services privately can be very expensive, and the older person may need to use his income from benefits to help meet these costs. There are further details about which benefits are available to older people in Chapter 8.

CHAPTER 3

Care in a care home

THIS CHAPTER COVERS THE FOLLOWING:

- When care in a care home may be necessary
- Why is the care needs assessment so important?
- Choosing a care home
- Information and contracts
- Care practices
- Staffing considerations
- The accommodation itself
- Meals in the home
- Leisure opportunities
- Religious activities
- Other important points to consider
- The move itself

Care in a residential care home is probably the first thing that people think of when they are trying to arrange support services for an older person. In fact, 400,000 older people live in residential care homes, while nearly 500,000 people receive home care services through social services, and a further estimated two million other people receive services privately at home. There is a great deal of support available either in people's own homes, or by moving into sheltered or extra care housing schemes.

However, the complexity of needs in an older person may mean that he can best be supported in a care home, and every effort should be made to make this a positive move. Most care homes provide excellent services, and look after residents thoughtfully, respectfully and with caring attention.

This chapter explains more about what you can expect from a care home, what to look for if you need to find one for an older person, and what questions you need to ask yourself and the older person who will be living in the care home. In reality, it is often the carers or families of the older person who look for the care home, and it can be a difficult decision to make on behalf of someone else. This chapter gives some guidance about what you need to think about when you are making this decision.

Details about the financial aspects of moving into a care home will be covered in the next chapter.

When care in a care home may be necessary

You may find that the older person is living at home in his own surroundings for many years, possibly with some informal support from friends, family or neighbours, or maybe some formal care from an agency or the local council. As time passes, he may find it less easy to cope, and it may gradually become necessary for you to consider care in a care home. However, where there is a reasonably steady decline in abilities like this, it is often easier to manage him with additional support from the informal care already in place, and so a care home may not always be necessary. Remember to find out about local support groups for carers. They will be able to tell you if there are services which could help you and the older person.

Alternatively, he may experience a sudden change in health which affects his ability to cope on his own. This might be an illness or health condition which worsens, or it could be a fall or accident which results in his being admitted to hospital.

Another possibility is that his dementia may intensify and mental capacity may decline, so he could be physically fit and active, but is in danger of harming himself or someone else because of his confusion. In these circumstances it is still possible to support an older person to live at home, but it is often these more extreme conditions which mean that a care home is the safest place for him.

If the needs of the older person are such that without 24-hour care he would be at significant risk, then care in a care home may be the most suitable way of supporting him. It may also be impossible to find a package of care at home which is intensive enough to support the older person. For example, if he needs a carer to visit more than four times a day, or during the night, a care home placement may be a necessary consideration.

The majority of care home placements are not arranged by the older person himself. This is often due to physical difficulties – arranging a care home generally means visiting and researching available places and, by definition, someone who needs a care home placement is not always able to do this. As a result, for people who have family or friends who can undertake the administration of finding a care home place, this job is nearly always passed on to them. You may be reading this guide because you know an older person who is in just this position. If the older person does not have family or friends, the social services of his local council will step in to make sure that he is placed into a suitable care home. The older person can ring social services himself to arrange to be assessed, but he can also be referred by his GP, or by any other voluntary services he is in contact with.

Although it is a difficult task to find a care home on behalf of someone else, and it can raise some difficult issues, it is very important to remember that the views and wishes of the older person do need to be taken into account, and that he may have reservations about going into a care home. In many cases, there are ways to support an older person which can be put in place in his own home and this is also the case if he has nursing or dementia care needs. So if the older person is reluctant to consider a move into a care home, consider all the other options carefully. If a social services assessment is arranged for the older person, it will be more clear what support could be offered by social services and health services, and what is available privately. It is also important to remember that someone cannot be forced into a care home, except in some circumstances under the Mental Health Act. While the older person has the capacity to make a decision, even if it considered unwise, he still has the right to make this choice.

However, if it has been decided that a care home move is the best option, and the older person is in agreement, what happens next? This can be quite a complex decision, but in many cases is one which needs to be made quickly; for example, if a crisis has occurred and the older person is no longer able to live safely on his own.

Why is the care needs assessment so important?

The needs assessment is the formal document which describes the care and support requirements specifically for an individual. You can arrange for an assessment to be carried out if you feel that your older relative is having difficulty managing on his own at home. This may be due to physical or mental health difficulties. The needs assessment is carried out by a social worker or care manager from the local council's social services department, and the form that he completes as a result of the assessment will highlight exactly what the care needs of the older person are. The assessment will also outline how these needs should be met. It may be that the social worker identifies a mixture of home support services for the older person, or he could highlight residential care as being the best option. The needs assessment is an essential document to have drawn up, because it will clarify exactly what is needed from a care home placement, if this has been highlighted as the most appropriate option. For example, if your mother has nursing care needs identified in the needs assessment, it will be necessary to find a home which provides this type of service. It sounds obvious, but there are many options to choose from! The more you can define exactly what you are looking for, the quicker and more straightforward your task will be, and you will be asking the right questions when you visit the care homes.

The care needs assessment is the responsibility of the social services department of the local council where the older person lives. If the older person is having difficulty with his daily living tasks and you think he could benefit from some support, you should contact the social services department and ask it to carry out the needs assessment. The department's contact details will be available in your local telephone directory, the local library or on the internet. You may have to briefly describe the older person's difficulties over the phone and the duty social worker will let you know how soon an assessment will take place. In many local authorities there is a waiting list for an assessment of need, but if you think that the older person's situation is urgent, you should make this clear, and ask for a more immediate assessment.

This care needs assessment should be carried out by the local council regardless of the financial circumstances of the older person. Some local councils avoid carrying out needs assessments for people who can afford to pay their own care home fees, but they have a duty to undertake this assessment, regardless of someone's income or capital. If the social worker asks questions about finances before carrying out a needs assessment, remind him that he has a duty to carry out a care needs assessment for anyone who appears to be in need of services. The local council is breaching government guidance and legislation if it refuses to carry out a needs assessment before it undertakes a financial assessment and you can make a complaint if you, or the older person, experience this. See Chapter 10 for more information about making a complaint if the older person has been refused an assessment of need.

Choosing a care home

So, a needs assessment has been carried out, and it identifies that the older person is in need of a care home placement; then what?

Firstly, it is very likely that the social worker will carry out a financial assessment of the older person, which considers his income, savings, investments and capital, including the value of his house. The financial assessment is carried out because those people who have a higher income, or who own a certain value of property or investments, are required to fund their own care home placement, using these savings and income. If financial support is given by the local authority, it will affect the options available when a care home is chosen. The next chapter of this guide looks in more detail at the financial assessment and how care home placements are funded.

It is also very likely that the social worker will give you, as the relative or friend of the older person, the responsibility of finding a care home which meets his care needs. Whenever there are family or friends able to help with this, the social worker will pass over the job. It means that he can concentrate on supporting those people who do not have available assistance. He should, however, give you adequate information for you to be able to complete this task. It is this information which is often lacking, and so relatives and carers are left to undertake this task with very little support or guidance.

There are over 20,000 care homes in the UK, but how do you choose between them? The types of care offered in care homes can vary. Some homes simply offer companionship and cooked meals for older people who are active, although this type of care is now limited. Residential care homes provide personal care for more dependent people. This might include help with washing, dressing, bathing, toileting needs, taking medicine and ensuring that an adequate diet is provided.

Other homes offer nursing care as well as personal care; for example, they may be able to assist people who:

- are unable to walk or stand on their own;

- have continence problems;

- are experiencing dementia; or

- have an illness or disability which is severe, and care can only be provided by a trained nurse.

There are a number of ways to find out about care homes in a particular area. If the older person has been assessed by a social worker, he should be given information about care homes, but this might not include details of all the homes in the local area. The Elderly Accommodation Counsel (tel: 020 7820 1343; www.housingcare.org) and the Commission for Social Care Inspection (tel: 0845 015 0120; www.csci.org.uk) can provide detailed information about care homes and all other types of accommodation for older people in the UK. There may also be books and directories in your local library that list available care homes, and a number of websites that give information about care homes. You need to be aware that some websites only list homes owned by one provider, so you may not obtain a complete list.

Having a copy of the completed needs assessment then becomes important, because this will specify exactly what care is needed from the care home. This is how you can begin to narrow down the options within a local area.

CASE STUDY

Mr Jones is 87. He lives on his own and has quite advanced dementia. He currently receives visits from care assistants every day, and they help him out of bed in the morning and to bed in the evening. He experiences a bad fall and is taken to hospital where a social worker undertakes a care needs review which involves the professional opinion of the psychogeriatrician. The review shows that Mr Jones is really in need of more constant care day and night, and that a care home is the best and safest environment for him to be in. He agrees and so do his daughter and son-in-law, who agree to help look for a suitable home in their local area.

Because a care needs assessment has been carried out, Mr Jones' daughter knows that she is looking for a care home which can cater for people who have dementia, and so she has a choice of four in their local area. Because Mr Jones owns his own home he will be self-funding his care home placement.

Mr Jones' daughter makes appointments to visit the four homes in the area, asking a series of questions and has a look around the homes herself. She also obtains the inspection reports from the Commission for Social Care Inspection website, so she can see how they are rated in the last inspection of each service. Three of the four homes have vacancies, and so the decision about which home to choose is made on the basis of a number of other factors; for instance, the weekly fees, whether the home is nearby to her house, how big the homes are, and what the staff are like. Mr Jones' daughter finds one that she likes and that has reasonable weekly rates, and arranges for her father to be moved into the home.

Mr Jones moves into the home ten days after his fall, and settles in quickly. The staff are friendly, there are other men in the home that he can talk to, and there is a garden he can sit in, which is really important for him as he is a keen gardener.

Moving into a care home may be a good opportunity for the older person to live in a different locality than his current house. Moving to be closer to family and other visitors may be one reason for such a move. If this is the case, and the older person is being funded by the local authority, it is the local authority which assessed the older person which continues to fund the care, and not the local authority where the new home is.

Once you have identified which home within a certain area you think may be appropriate, give the home a call to find out whether it has any vacancies. If it does, you should arrange to visit the home and meet the staff and manager, and check the facilities that are available. When visiting the home you may not have a lot of time to decide if it is suitable. It is a good idea to prepare the questions you want to ask before you get there and you may find the following headings are a good prompt of things to think about before visiting.

Information and contracts

All care homes should produce a 'statement of purpose' to help prospective residents and their families make a choice about the home. The statement should set out the home's objectives, philosophy of care, the services provided, the facilities, and the terms and conditions of the home. The home should also provide a service user's guide which includes:

- A statement of the home's aims and objectives

- The range of facilities and services available

- Details of any special care or facilities it offers; for example, care of people with a mental illness such as dementia, or care for people with particular cultural or religious needs

All care homes are subject to regular inspection by the Commission for Social Care Inspection (CSCI), which is the regulatory body of care homes and domiciliary care services in England. (In Wales this is the Care Standards Inspectorate (www.csiw.gov.uk) and in Scotland it is the Scottish Commission for the Regulation of Care (www.carecommission. com).) CSCI publishes inspection reports on all of the services it regulates, and you can obtain a copy of the latest inspection report for all of the care homes you are interested in. The reports are available to download from CSCI's website at www.csci.org.uk, or you can request a copy over the telephone on 0845 015 0120.

You should also check the terms of any contract you, or the older person, have to sign, and additionally find out:

- Under what circumstances could the home ask a resident to leave and how much notice will the home give?

- How much will the older person have to pay if he is away from the home for any reason?

- How much notice does a resident need to give to the home if he wants to move out?

- Does the home charge a non-refundable deposit? In what circumstances would it return a resident's deposit?

If there are any doubts about the terms of a home's contract or statement of purpose, you can take it to a Citizens Advice Bureau (contact details of local branches are available in your local telephone directory) or the Office of Fair Trading (tel: 0845 722 4499) for legal advice.

If the local council's social services are funding the care home placement for the older person, there should be a contract agreed between the local council and the care home. The contract should include the older person's care plan, which sets out how the home will meet his needs. You should read all the contracts that relate to the care of the older person to check the conditions and make sure that the care home is providing the correct level of care and support.

If you think that the contract you, or the older person, are being asked to sign by the care home is unfair, you may wish to read the guidance written by the Office of Fair Trading called '*Guidance on Unfair Terms in Care Home Contracts*', which can be purchased for £2 from The Stationery Office, PO Box 29, Norwich NR3 1GN, or downloaded free from www.oft.gov.uk. This gives examples of some unfair contractual terms, which can be used for comparison.

Care practices

You may wish to consider the type of care home the older person will want to live in:

- Are the friends and relatives along with the resident themselves involved in making decisions about the care provided?

- Is the care home suitable for the assessed care needs of the older person?

- Does the home have all the equipment necessary for the care of the older person; for example, hoists and easy-access baths and showers?

- Would the care home be able to cope with the care needs of the older person if they changed or increased? What would happen in these circumstances?

- How much control does the older person have over his care; for example, can he be in charge of his own medicine if he is able to manage this?

- Would the care home handle personal matters in a private and confidential way?

- Does the care home approach bathing, incontinence and giving medicine in a sensitive way?

- Can visitors be entertained at any time?

- Can visitors be seen in private?

- How much freedom is there to use the facilities and resources of the home?

- Can the resident leave the home when he wants?

- What services does the home provide; for example, physiotherapy, hairdressing and chiropody?

- Are the residents given the chance to take part in making decisions about general life in the care home?

- Is there a residents' committee?

- How will the care home make it possible for the resident to vote in elections?

- How will the care home regularly look at the care needs and how they are being managed? What will happen if changes to the care are needed?

- Can the resident and relatives take part in planning and reviewing the care provided?

- Can the resident look after his personal affairs (such as money and benefits), and does the home give enough privacy to do this?

- Can the resident spend time alone in his room if he wants to?

- Is there a choice of food available on the menu?

- How does the home serve meals? For example, do they use tablecloths and use tongs to serve cakes and sandwiches? Are the meals hot when they should be?

- Do residents have access to drinks when they need them?

- Can residents have meals served in their rooms?

Staffing considerations

During your visit it is important to consider the staff in the care home, as the older person will have contact with them on a daily basis, as will any visitors.

- Does it look as if there are enough members of staff?
- Do the staff seem too busy or do they have time to sit and spend time with residents?
- Do staff help residents to do things for themselves rather than doing things for them?
- Do you notice any members of staff talking with or assisting the residents?
- When the staff are assisting a resident, do they explain what they are going to do?
- Do the staff treat residents with respect?

You may want to ask the manager:

- Are the care staff expected to do domestic chores, such as cooking or cleaning, or are there separate staff for this?
- What training is available to the staff?
- Which staff have formal care qualifications? For example, do the care assistants have National Vocational Qualifications (NVQs) and are those involved in nursing Registered General Nurses (RGNs) or State Registered Nurses (SRNs)?
- Can any of the staff speak the resident's first language if this is not English?
- Are the staff trained in handling techniques; for example, turning and lifting residents? If not, the staff are not trained correctly.
- Is the care home compliant with the requirement to check members of staff under the Protection of Vulnerable Adults (POVA) and Criminal Records Bureau (CRB)?

- Are residents able to keep their own GP if they wish?

The accommodation itself

During your visit have a look at the facilities available in the home.

- Do the facilities seem well looked after?
- Do you like the decoration? Do you think that the older person would feel comfortable living there?
- Are the furnishings and fittings homely and in good condition?
- Are the bathrooms kept in a clean and hygienic state?
- How often are the other communal areas and individual bedrooms cleaned?
- Has the care home got up-to-date self-help equipment for the needs of the residents; for example, a lift, grab-rails, a minicom loop system for people with hearing difficulties, bathroom hoists, etc.?
- Is there easy access for wheelchairs or frames throughout the home?
- Can the residents take their pets?

Residents' rooms

- Are the rooms single or shared? (If they are shared, how is privacy achieved?)
- If there are shared rooms, do the residents choose to share? People in shared rooms have to make the choice to share; residents cannot be forced to share.
- Are any of the rooms en suite with bath, shower or toilet?
- Do the rooms smell fresh and clean?
- Can residents lock their rooms and, if this is not possible, is there a lockable drawer or cabinet within their rooms for their use?
- How many items of furniture or personal possessions are residents allowed to take with them?

- Can residents take their own televisions?

Communal rooms

- How many communal rooms are there?
- Are there different sitting areas, including quiet rooms?
- Is there a separate dining area?
- Are there toilets within easy reach of all parts of the home?
- Are there smoking and non-smoking areas?
- Are there plenty of call alarms to alert staff if assistance is needed?
- Is there a television in the communal room, and are suitable programmes shown on it?
- Do residents have access to a radio or other equipment?

The location of the home

- Is the care home near to family and friends?
- Is it convenient for shops, public transport and the GP?
- What is the surrounding area like?
- Is there an area for residents and visitors to sit outside if they wish to do so?

Meals in the home

These are an important aspect of the service provided in the care home:

- Can you look at copies of previous menus?
- Do the meals seem nutritious?
- Is the menu varied and interesting?
- Can residents choose what to eat?

- Are the residents involved in planning the menu?
- Can the home cater for residents if they have a special diet? Does this happen for any of the current residents?
- Is the dining area attractive and large enough?
- Can residents choose who to sit with?
- Can meals be brought to private rooms?
- Can guests share meals with the residents?
- Are there facilities for residents to make snacks and hot drinks?
- Will the home let you visit and have a meal with the current residents to see what it is like?
- Are extra portions available if residents still feel hungry?
- Are the meals served how you would expect them to be?
- Are the meals hot when they should be?

Leisure opportunities

- Are there any organised leisure activities; for example, arts and crafts, games, days out, etc.?
- Can residents choose to take part in these activities?
- How would residents be involved in planning and organising these activities?
- Can residents carry on doing the activities that they currently enjoy? Does the care home have the space and equipment to allow them to do this? Would the staff help?
- Would residents be able to take part in any activities outside the home by themselves?
- Would the care home help with transport or staff if it was needed by the resident?
- Does the care home have its own transport?
- Does the care home have its own garden?

Religious activities

- Will any religious needs of the residents be met; for example, do clergy call at the home, or can residents attend church?

- Does the home celebrate days or festivals; for example, St Patrick's Day, Diwali, Remembrance Sunday, Passover?

- Are there any volunteers who visit?

- Can friends or relatives help with activities?

- What services does the care home provide; for example, a television, library, the internet or hairdressing?

- Are there extra charges for any of these activities or services?

Other important points to consider

Does the home have a waiting list or a current vacancy available for the older person? This depends on whether the move into the care home is urgent. If the older person needs to move immediately, then waiting for a vacancy may not be practical. You can also ask the care home manager whether it is possible to arrange an extended visit or trial period to make sure that the care home really suits the older person. This is usually about four weeks, but can be for up to three months. If the council's social services department is funding the older person in the care home, the social worker involved in the older person's care should arrange a review meeting to make sure that the resident and the care home manager are happy that the older person's care needs are being met appropriately.

If the care home is being paid for by the local council (see the next chapter for more about paying for care home placements), the social worker or care manager should visit the older person in hospital or in his own home to make sure that he is happy with the choice of care home. They should also help relatives plan for the move into the care home.

The move itself

Once you have found a home that you are happy with and that you think the older person will settle into, you should make an appointment to see the manager of the home. The manager will also want to visit the older person, have a chat with him, and see for himself what his care needs are.

If all parties are happy with the proposed move, you will also be able to make arrangements at this meeting for the move into the care home. A date for the move should be set, and is likely to depend on whether the home has a vacancy or not. If any other assessments are needed, ask the manager whether they can be undertaken once the move has been made. Sometimes assessments for nursing care, etc. can be arranged once the resident is settled. Make sure that the home manager has got all of the correct contact details for you and the older person. Also, make sure that you clarify what can be brought into the home in terms of belongings and furniture.

CHAPTER 4

How to pay for care in a care home

THIS CHAPTER COVERS THE FOLLOWING:

- General principles
- Financial assessments by the local authority
- Occupational and private pensions
- Financial calculations for couples in care homes
- My parents still live together, so will they have to sell their jointly-owned home to pay for the care home fees?
- Payment for nursing care needs
- Full payment of care home fees by the NHS
- Arranging for a continuing care assessment
- Continuing care funding and a person's physical and mental healthcare needs
- Being denied continuing care funding
- Palliative care in care homes
- Care home placements funded by the local council
- Third party top-ups and how they affect the older person
- My mother has been financially assessed and she has between £13,000 and £21,500 in savings, capital and income. What does this mean?

- Self-funders paying the full cost of care home fees
- Contracts for care home placements funded by the individual
- Arranging the payment of fees
- Seeking advice about care fee planning

Paying for care in a care home is a complicated business, because there are many different possibilities and individual arrangements, and a great deal depends on the weekly cost of the care home itself. This chapter splits people into two groups – those whose care in a care home is paid for by the local authority, and those who pay for their own care, called 'self-funders'. The differences between them are explained in more detail throughout this chapter.

Many of the details in this chapter relate to England specifically, but there are general similarities between England, Wales and Scotland, although certain aspects are very different. Where there are major differences, these are referred to during the explanation. If you need specific advice about the arrangements for Wales and Scotland, you can seek advice from Age Concern Scotland (tel: 0845 125 9732; www.ageconcernscotland.org.uk) or Age Concern Wales (tel: 029 2043 1555; www.accymru.org.uk) or an advice agency such as Counsel and Care (tel: 0845 300 7585; www.counsel andcare.org.uk).

General principles

The system of paying for care homes in England and Wales starts with the premise that if an older person can afford to pay his own fees, he does so out of his own funds. Those individuals regarded as eligible for state support for their fees are people who are below a set threshold of income and capital savings. People who have nursing care needs are assessed by their local Primary Care Trust (PCT), and depending on the level of their nursing care needs, they receive a contribution per week towards the cost of the care home fees. Some people who have very intensive nursing care needs, and who are assessed as being eligible for what is called 'continuing care funding', will have all of their care home fees paid by their PCT. The full details of continuing care funding are set out on page 60 in this chapter of the guide.

In Scotland the system is different, because some services are provided free of charge. The NHS covers the cost of any nursing care received by the older person while he is in the care home. The local council, who assesses the older person's care needs, will provide care services free of charge. The charges the older person has to meet are for any additional services that he chooses to receive, and for his 'bed and board' costs (e.g. meals, washing, etc.).

Financial assessments by the local authority

Before starting to look for a care home, it is a good idea to obtain a care needs assessment, which is covered in more detail in Chapter 2. It will set out what someone's individual needs are and, as a result, what services are needed from a particular care home, and it will also narrow down the options available.

As stressed above, it is important that a care needs assessment is carried out before a financial assessment is completed. The local council is not able to deny an older person a care needs assessment on the basis that he is able to afford to pay his own care home fees. The council has a duty to assess everyone who appears to be in need of care. You can request an assessment of need by contacting the duty social work team in the social services department of the local council where the older person currently lives. If the older person is currently in hospital, the staff there will help you to do this. Read Chapter 3 for a more detailed explanation of the needs assessment.

After the needs assessment has been completed, the social worker will arrange for a financial assessment of the older person, which will establish how much financial support the local council will be able to offer to him. You can be present at this assessment, if the older person wishes for this, or if he needs help from you to understand what he is being asked.

A financial assessment is carried out because residential care services are not free if individuals own assets or have savings. The financial assessment will work out how much the older person owns in terms of his savings, investments and property, and will establish how much money he will be expected to contribute to the cost of his care home fees.

Before the social worker arrives, he should tell you and the older person what financial information he will need, along with any supporting documents he will need to see. This means that you can help prepare for the assessment, so that everything is ready before the social worker arrives to complete the assessment. The financial assessment will ask a number of questions about the older person's monthly income, his savings in accounts, his shares and investments, and any capital he owns, like a house or other property. The questions should be asked of the individual only, and this is really important. If it is your mother going into a care home, your father is under no obligation to provide details of money, savings or investments in his name. People have sometimes been caught out by this, as once a local council knows how much money a couple have between them, it often pursues a spouse for additional money, which otherwise would be provided by the council. This is called being a 'liable relative' and there are more details about this later on in this chapter. Only the income, savings and capital owned by the person going into the care home should be taken into account.

The financial assessment will take all assets into account, and will establish what needs to be provided by the individual. If the older person has less than £13,000 in capital and savings, the full cost of the care home will be met by the local council. In this situation all of his weekly income will be taken as part of the payment for the care home, apart from a weekly amount of £20.45, known as a 'Personal Expenses Allowance'. This can be used to pay for any personal items needed. For some people who have made modest savings, they may be eligible for Pension Savings Disregard, which is worth up to £5.25 a week, and which is added to the level of the Personal Expenses Allowance. There are more details about this later on in this chapter.

If the older person has between £13,000 and £21,500 in savings, investments or property, a proportion of the care home fees will need to be met by the individual, and the local council will pay the remainder. Again, any income the older person receives from pensions and benefits will be taken into account and will also be used to meet the cost of the care home. Some types of income are not included in the calculation because they are known as 'disregarded income'. These include:

- The mobility component of Disability Living Allowance

- (War Pension Scheme) mobility supplement (this is an additional payment to a war veteran if an injury he sustained on service means that he has serious difficulty in walking)
- Special War Widow's Pension
- Some charitable payments
- Pension Savings Disregard

The council will work out what is known as a 'tariff income', which means that for every £250 between £13,000 and £21,000 the older person will be regarded as having £1 a week income.

If the total savings, investments and property owned by the older person is worth more than £21,500, he will have to meet the full cost of the care home fees. If the older person's capital is less than £21,500 but his weekly income is above the level of the care home fees and Personal Expenses Allowance added together, he will be expected to meet the full cost of the care home fees from this income.

Occupational and private pensions

If the older person is moving to a care home leaving his spouse or partner in his previous residence, half of the occupational or private pension must be disregarded by the council in his financial assessment.

Financial calculations for couples in care homes

If both of your parents are moving into a care home at the same time, the local council will assess them as separate individuals with separate finances. This means that they can have savings of £21,500 each and the local council will have responsibility for payment of the care home fees, providing their weekly incomes are not above the care home fees level. If they have joint savings and investments, these will be split in half for the purposes of the financial assessment.

If they both move into the same care home and have separate living arrangements, they can still be treated by the Department for Work and

Pensions as having separate finances for the purposes of claiming Pension Guarantee Credit; that is, they will not be classed as a 'couple'. If the Department for Work and Pensions treats your parents as a couple for the calculation of Pension Guarantee Credit, you may wish to contact an advice service such as Counsel and Care (tel: 0845 300 7585; www.counsel andcare.org.uk) for further advice.

My parents still live together, so will they have to sell their jointly-owned home to pay for the care home fees?

No, it is laid out very clearly in charging guidance for local authorities that they must not take into account the value of a home if a dependent relative or spouse is still living there. This means that only the savings and investments in the name of the person moving into care will be taken into account. Any joint savings and investments will be split so that 50 per cent is taken into account.

Payment for nursing care needs

Nursing and healthcare is provided free in England, Wales and Scotland on the NHS. This is applicable wherever the nursing care is provided, so that if an older person lives in a care home and he is receiving nursing care, the NHS should cover the cost of this.

If the older person has nursing care needs, they will have been identified in the care needs assessment carried out by the social worker. If it was established in this assessment, the older person will be referred to a nurse, who will complete an additional assessment to establish in more detail what these nursing needs are, and what care is required to meet them. The cost of nursing care in a care home is met by a weekly contribution by the NHS, which is made to the care home itself, and not to the individual. The level of contribution depends on the older person's level of nursing care needs. This contribution is not means-tested, so he will receive it regardless of his income, capital and savings. This contribution is known as a 'Registered Nursing Care Component' (RNCC).

The nurse who carries out the RNCC assessment will establish more precisely what the nursing needs are, and will place the needs into one of three categories:

1. **Low needs** require minimal registered nursing care input. They are paid at a rate of **£40** per week.

2. **Medium needs** require care from a registered nurse at least daily but the individual has a stable and predictable physical or mental condition. Medium nursing care is provided at **£83** per week.

3. **High needs** are defined as very complex. High needs would require 'mechanical, technical and/or therapeutic interventions throughout 24 hours' and the individual has 'unstable or unpredictable mental health'. The high band is provided at **£133** per week.

If the care home fees of the older person are paid by the local council, the RNCC payment reduces the council's level of contribution. Any payment made will not reduce the assessed financial contribution made by the older person, or any third party top-up made. If the older person pays the care home fees himself, the RNCC contribution will reduce the level of fees by the relevant amount.

Full payment of care home fees by the NHS

There are circumstances in which the NHS will cover the full cost of an older person's care home fees, if his health needs meet certain criteria. This includes mental health needs as well as physical health needs. This is called 'continuing healthcare', and is generally referred to as 'continuing care funding'. Continuing care funding can also be received if the older person is receiving his care at home, although it is rare for this to be arranged.

People are entitled to receive continuing care funding depending on the nature, complexity, intensity or unpredictability of their healthcare needs. Individual PCTs are required to have criteria which set out exactly what care needs will be met in their particular area. It is currently the case that every PCT will have slightly different criteria, although there is a requirement that these be based on national guidance from the Department of Health. However, at the time of writing this guide, there is an expectation that the Department of Health will publish new national criteria which will be used by all PCTs for assessing who is eligible to receive continuing care funding. This will mean that there is a greater level of consistency across the country, as all people will be assessed on the same basis.

The national guidance used currently states that continuing care funding is provided according to:

- The nature, complexity, intensity, or unpredictability of the individual's healthcare needs (and any combination of these which requires regular supervision by a member of the NHS multi-disciplinary team).

- Whether the individual's needs require routine use of specialist healthcare equipment under supervision of NHS staff.

- Whether the individual has a rapidly deteriorating or unstable medical, physical or mental health condition and requires regular supervision by a member of the NHS multi-disciplinary team.

- Whether the individual is in the final stages of a terminal illness and is likely to die in the near future.

It is not just the severity of the condition which should be taken into consideration, but the type of care required to meet the needs resulting from the health condition.

If someone is assessed as needing this type of nursing care, the NHS in the local area will pay for the full cost of the care home fees, regardless of the income, capital and savings of the individual. If an older person receives this funding, he is unlikely to have much influence over the location of the care – the care managers involved will choose a care home which can meet the needs of the individual, and at a charged rate which is acceptable to the PCT. If you, as a family member of the resident, are likely to have difficulty visiting the older person as a result of the location of the care home, you should raise this with the care manager and ask him to reconsider the location, stressing the importance of family visits. If you are a close friend, you can also argue that visits from you are important to the older person's emotional and psychological well-being.

Continuing care funding is notoriously difficult to obtain. In 2006, 25,000 people were granted the funding, but it is thought that 100,000 people should have received it (source: Age Concern). If you feel that the older person's needs may mean that he is eligible for the funding, you should contact a social worker or the doctor or nurse who is currently in charge of his care. They will be able to give advice on how to obtain an assessment.

CASE STUDY

Mrs Bell has been resident in a care home for a year. When she originally moved into the care home she was in the early stages of dementia but she has developed more severe symptoms in recent weeks. She also has very severe arthritis which means that she cannot walk or bear her own weight. She requires ongoing pain control to remain comfortable. Her family requests a review of her nursing care needs, because they feel that her requirements are so constant that she should be moved from the middle band of RNCC, and that she is eligible for continuing care funding. The registered nurse in the care home reassesses Mrs Bell, and she is found to be eligible for the full continuing care funding. Her arthritis is taken into account, as well as her mental health needs caused by the dementia, as her needs are never predictable, and she requires 24-hour supervision. Because the care home she is living in is able to meet her needs as assessed in the new assessment, she is able to remain in the same home. The PCT confirms that it is happy to pay the charges in this home.

Arranging for a continuing care assessment

If the older person is currently receiving hospital treatment, the doctor or nurse in charge of his care will be able to arrange for a continuing care assessment to take place. This could be completed by a medical consultant or doctor; ward nurse or specialist nurse; a speech and language or occupational therapist. If the older person lives in a care home, ask the home manager or a member of the nursing staff and they will be able to assist you, or complete an assessment themselves.

The assessment should look at different areas of the medical and personal needs relating to the particular health condition/s experienced, such as:

- Personal care needs (e.g. the ability to carry out washing, bathing and dressing)

- Continence, both urine and bowel (including the management of incontinence)

- Tissue viability and the risk of pressure sores

- Clinical background (past health needs and the care and support that was required)

- Mental health needs (e.g. dementia, depression and the behaviours and treatment relating to these)

- Medication (the ability to manage its safe use)

- Safety (is the individual at risk or is he a risk to somebody else?)

- Pain (the level of care needed to manage it with dignity)

- Nutrition and fluids (what care does the older person need to ensure that he receives adequate levels of these?)

- Mobility (the ability to walk or move about without support)

- Communication (how is the patient able to express his needs or process information?)

- The overall risk to the older person as a result of his condition and the above factors

If you ask for an assessment for the older person, but you do not agree with the outcome of it, you can ask for a review to be conducted. You will have to give good reasons why you think that the nursing care needs are intense, complex or unpredictable. You may want to see specialist advice before you ask for a review, by calling an agency such as Counsel and Care (tel: 0845 300 7585; www.counselandcare.org.uk).

Continuing care funding and a person's physical and mental healthcare needs

A recent Health Service Ombudsman report made clear that NHS continuing care is not just for those patients with physical healthcare needs. Continuing care should also be available to people with mental health needs, including those relating to dementia, if the level of needs meet the local criteria set out by the PCT. For example, it may be that the person with dementia is physically mobile, but his condition requires intensive supervision to prevent his being harmed or harming others. Or, the advancement of the dementia might mean that the person requires regular repositioning, personal hygiene care, feeding and provision of fluids. The same continuing care criteria and assessment should be completed to assess the needs of someone with dementia. This assessment should include the opinion of a psychiatrist or other mental health professional.

If this has not happened or you have been told that the older person is not entitled to continuing care because he has dementia without a full assessment being carried out, you should consider raising a complaint on his behalf. You may also wish to contact the Alzheimer's Society (tel: 0845 300 0336; www.alzheimers.org.uk) for further information and support in obtaining continuing care for an older person with dementia.

Being denied continuing care funding

If the older person has received an assessment for continuing care funding, but has been refused the funding, you should ask to see the assessment and criteria on which the decision has been based. If you are denied a copy of the completed assessment, your local PCT's Patient Advice and Liaison Service (PALS), an independent advocate, the Independent Complaints Advocacy Service (tel: 0845 120 7111; www.cppih.org/icas.html) or an advice service, such as Counsel and Care (tel: 0845 300 7585; www.counselandcare.org.uk), may be able to support you to obtain it.

You can ask for a review of the decision, firstly by contacting the professional who carried out the initial assessment, stating why you think the older person should receive the funding. If a review is denied, or if you are still unhappy with the decision, you can raise the case as a complaint, writing to the Chief Executive of the PCT who made the decision.

Palliative care in care homes

It may be that the older person is nearing the end stage of his life due to a terminal illness, and therefore needs palliative care. This is care that is funded free of charge by the NHS, and can be provided in hospital, in a hospice, in a care home, and in someone's own home. The care is provided by social care professionals and by specialist doctors and nurses who are trained specifically in this area. Palliative care services are designed to keep the patient comfortable and ensure that he has the best quality of life possible.

Local PCTs have individual eligibility criteria for the funding, which are often quite restrictive about what point in the terminal illness the person's life is considered to be at the end stage. If you think that someone you know may be eligible for palliative care, talk to the consultant in charge of his care. Although this may be a difficult conversation, it is important for the consultant to confirm that the person is at the end stage so that it is clear that he is entitled to palliative care.

Care home placements funded by the local council

If the older person is not receiving continuing care funding, and is being funded in the care home by the local council (because he is below the capital limit of £21,500), the family will usually be given the task of finding a suitable care home for the older person. If there are no family or friends available to help find a care home, the social worker will undertake a search for a suitable placement.

If you have been charged with this task, you should be given a copy of the assessed care needs, which would have been identified in the needs assessment the social worker carried out.

There are several things which you need to consider if you are in this position:

- **The standard rate that the council is offering:** This is the amount of money that the council will pay for a care home. The standard rate has to be realistic, so that you are able to actually buy a place in a care home which meets all of the older person's assessed needs. It is very important to remember that it has to be a realistic figure – the council cannot arbitrarily set a figure which does not relate to the market in the local area. You should be automatically informed by the social worker who undertook the assessment of the older person what the council's standard rate is; if not, you need to ask him. You cannot begin to search for a care home unless you know what this financial restriction might be. The social worker will be able to give you this information.

- **How to find a home which meets this standard rate:** The social worker who assessed the older person should give you a list of care homes in the local area which meet the council's standard rate. Not all of the care homes will have vacancies, however, and some of them will be designed for needs which are different from the older person's. You will need to visit the homes which can meet the assessed needs (e.g. the nursing homes on the list if that is what you are looking for). Use the checklists in Chapter 3 of this guide to help you decide which home you like best. It is worth ringing the home before you visit to double check that it will accept the standard rate offered by the council.

- **What to do if there are no homes available:** Sometimes there may be no vacancies in the homes which accept the local council's standard rate, or you may find that the suitable care homes have no vacancies; for example, there are no dementia care homes on the list which have a vacancy. In this situation, the council must increase its standard rate so that a care home place can be found.

For instance, there are no care homes which meet the assessed needs of Mrs Ross in a particular area. All the care homes which accept £400 are found to be full. Her daughter finds a care home which charges £430 per week and which meets all of the assessed needs. The local council must therefore provide £430 per week for this care.

If this happens, the council can place the resident in the more expensive home, but it can then require the patient to be moved into a cheaper home once a cheaper placement becomes available.

- **What are the options if you do not like the homes which accept the standard rate?** You have looked around at all of the homes which accept the standard rate and the older person's care needs, and you do not like any of them, or you do not think that the older person will settle in them. Unfortunately, you have limited options. You can either find a care home which you do like, and find a third party to pay the difference in cost (as it is likely to be more expensive), or the older person has to move into one of the homes which you do not like. It comes down to whether the reason for the other homes being unsuitable is because of preference or because of a care need. If the homes are not suitable because you do not like them, this is a preference. If it is a need (i.e. the care homes actually cannot provide the care that the older person requires), this must be looked at by the local council, and you can ask the social services department to adjust its standard rate. There are more rules about third parties which are covered below.

If you have found a home that you are happy the older person will settle into, you can start to make arrangements for the move. This will involve liaising with the care home manager, social worker and the discharge team at the hospital (if the older person is currently in hospital). You should arrange with the manager of the care home for the invoice for the care home to be sent directly to the local council for payment.

Q What money do residents get to spend on personal items?

A Care home residents who have their full fees paid by the local council are allowed a weekly amount of £20.45 which they are able to keep back from their pension and other benefits. This is called the Personal Expenses Allowance, and can be spent on anything they want (e.g. clothes, newspapers, haircuts, etc.). The money should not be used to buy additional services which are required by the older person (e.g. chiropody), as these should be provided and paid for either by the local council as part of the care package, or by the NHS if they are health services.

Third party top-ups and how they affect the older person

'Third party top-ups' is the name given to an additional weekly payment made by friends and family for a care home placement. The amount literally 'tops up' the amount that the local authority will pay for a care home, so that the older person can move into a care home of his choice. The weekly amount could be anything up to £150 per week, depending on the fees of the care home of choice.

There are some important facts to remember about third party top-ups:

- They are beneficial because they open up more choice about which care home is available. More expensive care homes may provide more services, have different types of décor and may be more luxurious. They should still provide the same quality of care available in a care home which accepts a lower fee.

- Third party top-ups can only be charged when the older person or his family is choosing a care home which is more expensive, and where there are other homes available which meet the assessed needs. So, it means that if you cannot find a care home which meets the local council's standard rate, you should not be a charged a third party top-up – the council should raise its rate.

- If you are considering providing a third party top-up for the older person, think carefully about whether this is affordable in a long-term arrangement. The average length of stay in a care home is two years – is this affordable for you? Remember that if the third party top-up cannot be paid, it is likely that the older person will be moved to a cheaper home if the council becomes responsible for the fees.

- Make sure that the local council pays all of the care home fees in full, including the amount of the third party top-up, and then invoices you separately for the third party top-up. The care home should not invoice you directly. This is important so that the council knows how many people have to provide a third party top-up in your area.

- When you are deciding whether you can afford to pay, be prepared for any increase in the fees to be passed directly to the person paying the top-up. A care home can raise its fees once or, in some cases, twice a year.

My mother has been financially assessed and she has between £13,000 and £21,500 in savings, capital and income. What does this mean?

For every £250 or part of £250 which is owned by your mother, she will be assumed to have a £1 a week income. This amount will be added to the assessment of the weekly income. Therefore, your mother will need to pay a weekly amount towards the care home fees from her capital savings, until they reach the value of £13,000. In practice, this is likely to mean that the local council pays the majority of the care home fees with a weekly contribution from your mother. She should still keep the weekly Personal Expenses Allowance of £20.45. When the savings reach £13,000 the fees of the care home should be met entirely by the local council.

If you are involved in choosing the care home for the older person, and he is paying a contribution towards the care home fees because he is in the bracket above, it is important to choose a care home which will accept the local council's standard rate. This is because, if the older person does become entirely supported by the local council, the social services department will check that the care home is charging a rate that is acceptable to it. If the older person is living in a home which charges significantly more than the council's standard rate, it is likely that the council will insist that he moves into a cheaper home. Therefore, to save the difficulties and upheaval involved in an accommodation move, it may be better if an initial move into a home is one where the council's standard rate is accepted.

Self-funders paying the full cost of care home fees

The term 'self-funder' is used to describe people who receive no financial support from the local council. They entirely fund their care home placement using their savings and capital, because together their assets are worth over £21,500. Or, if their weekly income is more than the cost of the care home fees, they will also pay the full cost of the placement.

The process of choosing a home should be followed as has been previously outlined in other chapters and above, making sure that the home chosen can meet all of the assessed needs, and that both you and the older person are happy with it. As in the other circumstances, it is likely that the family of the older person will need to find the care home placement, as there is limited support available from local councils for self-funded residents.

Someone who is a self-funder essentially has a free choice of care home, the main restriction being the budget available to spend.

If you have been given the responsibility of finding a care home placement for an older person who is a self-funder, there are a number of things you need to consider:

- **The care needs of the older person:** It is important that the older person has received a care needs assessment from a social worker at his local council. The older person is still entitled to receive this assessment, even if he will be paying for and arranging his own care home placement. This care needs assessment will set out what he needs from a care home, which in turn will help you identify which care homes are most suitable for him.

  You can find care homes which are suitable for his needs by contacting the Elderly Accommodation Counsel (tel: 020 7820 1343; www.housingcare.org) or the Commission for Social Care Inspection (tel: 0845 015 0120; www.csci.org.uk). The social worker who undertakes the assessment of need should also be able to give you a list of approved care homes in your local area.

  When you have found a care home which you would like to place the older person in, you should arrange to speak to the manager of the care home. He will make a visit to see the older person, to assess his needs, and to check whether the home is able to meet those needs.

  If it is agreed that the home will be able to meet the care needs, a care plan should be arranged between the resident and the care home, and a contract should be drawn up. You and the older person should preferably receive both of these documents in writing before he moves into the care home. However, sometimes this is not possible if a move is urgent. If this is the case, you should make sure that you receive them both as soon as possible. Check that what you have agreed has been written into the care plan and contract, and that you are happy with both before they are signed. If the older person has mental capacity, he will need to sign the contract himself. If you are the representative of someone who does not have capacity, a family member can sign on behalf of the resident. For more details about mental capacity and how to establish whether an older person has the ability to make decisions for himself, please see the relevant sections in Chapters 5 and 6. It is important that you make sure that all the services you want the older person to receive are written in either or both documents, as these can be used to challenge the care provided if you feel it is not meeting the standard you agreed.

- **The amount of capital available to use:** This is important to consider because it affects how long term the care home placement is likely to be. For instance, if your father owns a house worth £150,000, he will be required to use this capital to pay for his care (provided that there are no other dependent relatives living in the property). Because the first £21,500 is not taken into account, he effectively has £128,500 to spend on his care. If the care home costs £450 per week, it will cost £23,400 per year, and the costs are likely to increase each year with inflation. Consider also where his spending money will come from – it may be from his benefits, pension or other income.

An important consideration is whether the capital available is very close to the upper limit of £21,500. Remember that when someone has capital of below this amount the local council has the responsibility of picking up the costs of the care home placement. The local council is unlikely to continue paying for a care home which is above its usual rate per week and, therefore, it may ask the older person to move into a cheaper home. It may be better and less disruptive, therefore, if the older person is placed in a care home which meets the usual rate of the local council, and that way when the council starts paying the cost of the fees, he will not have to move home.

- **When a property is involved:** If the older person owns a property worth more than £21,500 and he lives alone, he will be required to use the value of his property to pay for the cost of his care home placement. There are some important considerations to remember if you are helping to arrange this placement on behalf of the older person, and he has several rights and entitlements which the local council must adhere to.

Firstly, when he moves into the care home, he is entitled to have the first 12 weeks of the fees disregarded, if he has less than £21,500 in savings other than his property. This means that the local council will contribute towards the care home fees (usually up to its standard rate), even if the older person will be paying the full cost himself after this initial 12-week period. This is designed so that the property does not need to be sold immediately on his moving into the care home, and it allows for any changes in his care needs after he has initially moved in, or if he decides to move back out of the care home into his property.

You, and the older person, have two options when you are considering what to do next. The local council of the older person will also be able to give more guidance about these options.

- The older person can choose to sell his home to pay for his care. This is likely to mean that relatives and other friends will be involved. Once the property is sold, the older person will use this funding to pay the care home fees until the money has run down to the capital limit of £21,500. (This is the capital limit for the financial year 2007–08, but it will alter in subsequent years. To find out the current rate, please contact Counsel and Care's advice service on 0845 300 7585 or email advice@counseland care.org.uk.)

- If the older person does not wish to sell his house, the local council can offer a deferred payments option. This is where the charges of the care home will be paid by the local council until the death of the resident or until he moves out of the care home. After this time the property will need to be sold, and the money owed to the local council paid from the proceeds of the sale. The benefit of this option is that the property does not have to be sold while the older person is still alive, which can often be quite distressing for him. The local council will place a charge on the property.

- **Deprivation of capital:** It is important to remember that there are also rules surrounding what is regarded as 'deprivation of capital'. This is where someone is found to have deliberately used or given away money in order to avoid paying care home fees. It means that the older person cannot give away large sums of money, transfer the ownership of the property, or spend his money on something which is not necessary (e.g. an expensive painting). If this happens, he will be assessed as though he still has that money, and he will have to pay the care home fees himself. The Department for Work and Pensions can look retrospectively through records, even beyond seven years. In looking back they will decide whether a gift of property or cash was a deliberate deprivation to avoid care home fees. This means that if an amount of money was given to grandchildren many years before care was needed, the council should not regard it as deliberate. However, if this money was given two months before a move into a care home, it would be regarded as deliberate deprivation.

Contracts for care home placements funded by the individual

If the older person is funding his own placement in the care home, he should expect to sign a contract with the care home manager, outlining what the expectations of both parties are. The contract that is made with the care home should determine the following:

- The basis of the stay; for example, whether it is permanent, temporary or a trial stay

- Information about the room that the resident will be occupying

- The care and services, including arrangements for meals, drinks and laundry

- The fees or charges and how they are calculated, how often and when the fees are due

- Who is responsible for paying the fees

- Whether there are additional services to be paid for

- The resident's rights and entitlements

- The care home's rights and obligations

- How to make a complaint if you, or the older person, are not satisfied with the care provided

- The period of notice required by either party before being able to terminate the contract or move out of the care home

- How the care home will meet any special requirements, such as dietary or religious needs

- How any changes to the care needs will be managed

- How the resident's money and valuables will be secured, and who holds the responsibility for insuring them

- What liability insurance the care home has

- What the individual will be charged to hold his place if he is away from the care home temporarily

- How he can keep his property safe and secure

Be wary of the following being omitted from a contract – you should make sure that you clarify:

- How much the fees are, how often they are paid and who is responsible for the payment

- If the care home is excluded from liability for causing death or injury

- If the care home excludes itself from providing a particular service

- If the care home is excluded from looking after property and possessions of the residents

- If the care home excludes itself from responsibility if clothes are damaged in the laundry

- If the care home is allowed to make significant changes to its services without consulting residents or their relatives

- Whether the care home can change a resident's room without consulting him

- If staff can enter rooms without the consent of the resident

- Whether the care home has the right to keep or dispose of property or possessions

- The terms surrounding payment of the care home fees if the resident dies

No contract should be signed until all parties are happy with the arrangements, and only after it has been clarified exactly what services the home will provide.

If you are unhappy with any aspect of the contract the older person is asked to sign, you could contact the Commission for Social Care Inspection (tel: 0845 015 0120; www.csci.org.uk) to discuss it.

Arranging the payment of fees

The contract should provide details of how the care home fees are to be paid. If the care home placement is being paid for in full by the local council, it will make arrangements directly with the care home. If some of the fees are paid for by the local council, but there are outstanding charges which will be paid from a third party top-up, the council should arrange to pay the net amount directly to the care home. The council should then invoice the resident or a third party for their contribution. That way, if there are any changes to the fees, the local council will maintain full funding responsibility while other arrangements and increases in contribution are arranged by the other parties. The Charging for Residential Accommodation Guidance (CRAG), which governs how all care home payments should be arranged, states that unless all parties (the care home manager, the resident and any third parties) agree otherwise, the council should pay the full fees directly to the care home and invoice the resident for his assessed contribution (including the third party contribution).

Seeking advice about care fee planning

As the system for funding care home placements is so complex, there are a number of sources of advice you can contact to seek more information and guidance. Several agencies can advise about the financial products on the market to help people invest money to pay for future care home fees. Sometimes if money is invested in payment plans, it is possible to maintain ownership of a property if someone wants to keep this intact as an inheritance or if the older person does not want to have to sell the property to pay for his care. You can obtain advice from Saga's Care Funding Advice Service (tel: 0800 056 8153; www.saga.co.uk/finance), NHFA (tel: 0800 998 833; www.nhfa.co.uk) or IFA Care (tel: 01562 822 955; www.ifacare.co.uk).

CHAPTER 5

Being a carer

THIS CHAPTER COVERS THE FOLLOWING:

- Who is a carer?
- What rights do I have as a carer?
- Where do I start?
- Your right to information
- Your right to an assessment of need
- Delays in assessment
- Your right to request flexible working
- Support services available to carers
- Being charged for support services
- Direct payments for carers
- Welfare benefits available to carers
- When can I make a decision for the older person?
- What if I am reading this before October 2007?
- Organisations which can provide further help to carers

Who is a carer?

Many people are carers in the UK – around six million – which is nearly a tenth of the population, and it is likely that there are many more than this figure who are not known about and who do not identify themselves as carers. Someone can become a carer overnight if a relative or friend has a crisis which means that he is no longer able to look after himself without support. Some people are carers only for a short time while the person gets better or moves into other supported accommodation, and other people can be carers for most of their lives.

You are a carer if you provide care for a dependent friend or relative. This could be a young child, someone with a physical or learning disability, or an older person, such as a parent, grandparent or neighbour. Some carers provide small amounts of help, such as taking a person to the shops, helping him with his food or getting him out of bed, and other carers provide full-time support, both day and night.

Carers who come into certain categories are entitled to particular benefits and entitlements as a result of their caring role. These are looked at more closely in this chapter.

Becoming a carer can affect a person's life in a very dramatic way. It can disrupt his family life, particularly if he becomes a carer at a time of crisis. It can affect his working life, as he may need flexible hours, or in some cases he may have to give up work altogether. Carers also have to be careful that they do not harm their own physical or mental health in their caring role; for example, by lifting someone without proper training. There is also an increasing number of people taking on a caring role while also being older and potentially in need of care themselves. Some older couples may have to provide physical and personal care for each other. However, there are options available to carers to organise respite care, welfare benefits are available from the government, and there are new laws in place to protect employees from having to give up work because of inflexible hours. All of these are looked at further on in this chapter.

It is also easy to confuse an informal carer, such as a friend or relative, with a formal care worker, who is a paid member of staff in a care home or care agency. This chapter looks at the needs of, and services available to, informal carers.

KEY FACTS AND FIGURES

- About six million people in the UK are carers.
- Carers save the economy the equivalent of another NHS each year – an average of £10,000 per carer.

- Over three million carers are also in employment.
- 1.25 million people provide over 50 hours of care per week.
- People providing high levels of care are twice as likely to be permanently sick or disabled.
- Over one million people care for more than one person.
- 58 per cent of carers are women and 42 per cent are men.
- Every year over two million people become carers.

Source: Carers UK, March 2007

What rights do I have as a carer?

Being a carer entitles you to a range of support, some of which is available through your local social services department, and some of which you can arrange yourself. It is important to remember that if you are a carer, you have your own needs, and that they are separate and just as important as the needs of the person you are caring for.

Where do I start?

If you are reading this guide, it is likely that you have become a carer because your elderly mother, father, friend, partner or relative has become frail, and is therefore in need of some assistance from you, or you are helping him to arrange this support from elsewhere.

If you are in this position, you should first read Chapter 1 of this guide, which talks about the types of care available to older people. Use this to try to work out with the older person which type of services he may like to put in place, and contact a social worker at your local council to ask for an assessment of need, which looks at the care and support needs of the person who requires care. After this assessment of need, if someone is entitled to services from the council, these will be arranged and provided. If the assessment establishes that the person needs support, but that this is not to be provided by the council, the social worker who undertakes the assessment should provide the necessary information so that the services can be arranged privately by the individual through a care agency, or other similar service.

It may be that once support services have been put in place for the older person, your role as a carer is easier because you will not be the only support in place.

However, today's social services departments are increasingly strict about whom they will support with services. What are called low level services, those which provide light support with day-to-day tasks, such as cleaning, shopping and preparing food, are very scarce from these departments. Many no longer provide this type of service because they concentrate their resources on those older people with the highest needs. It is likely, therefore, that if this is the sort of service that you think needs to be put in place for the older person, then this will have to be arranged privately. However, you should still seek an assessment from social services, because this will identify what needs the older person has.

You can find information about available services for the older person through the social worker, or by contacting an advice agency, such as Counsel and Care (tel: 0845 300 7585; www.counselandcare.org.uk), or through your local Age Concern office (its details will be in your local telephone directory). Age Concern will be able to tell you what services are available in your local area.

CASE STUDY

Mr Evans and his wife are both in their early 80s and live in their own home, where they manage very well. Mrs Evans has recently been diagnosed with the early stages of dementia. She needs occasional supervision with tasks such as making hot drinks, because she can be forgetful, and Mr Evans is concerned that she will hurt herself. She is capable of making decisions about most things, but Mr Evans wants to know what will happen if her dementia gets worse. He also wants to know what support services are available in their local area.

Mr Evans contacts his local social services department, and arranges for a social worker to visit and assess their support needs. The social worker finds that both of them have care needs, and that Mr Evans also needs support to help him in his caring role.

The council is not able to provide these services to Mr and Mrs Evans because their needs are not currently high enough, but the social worker does tell Mr Evans what is available in the local area, so that he can arrange services privately. He organises for a carer to visit for an afternoon twice a week so that he can play bowls with his friends, and do the food shopping.

Your right to information

As a carer you will need access to a large range of information. This will be necessary so that you can arrange the care services for the older person you are helping to support, but you will also need information about benefits, for both you and the older person, so you will need to know what your own rights as a carer are, and you will need to know where to go to apply for these rights.

The Carers (Equal Opportunities) Act 2004 has established in law a number of measures which are designed to help carers achieve these rights. The Act means that a local authority has a responsibility to make sure that you receive all of the information that you are entitled to. As a carer you can approach the local authority at any time for this information; the person you are caring for does not have to be receiving services from the local authority, and neither do you.

Your right to an assessment of need

In order to establish whether you are eligible for council-provided services, a social worker or care manager should carry out an assessment of your needs and requirements for support, to ensure that you can continue caring and have some time to yourself. This is called a 'carer's assessment'. This assessment will look at a variety of things to see how you are being affected by your caring role.

Your carer's assessment can be carried out at the same time as the needs assessment for the cared-for person, if he is also having an assessment. (It is important to remember that he does not have to have an assessment for you, as the carer, to receive one.) Alternatively, you may wish to have your assessment carried out separately, so that you can speak more openly to the social worker about your needs without fear of causing distress for the person you care for. Ask your social worker for a separate assessment in confidence. Before you have an assessment you may like to think about the following:

- Are you able to get enough sleep, or is it disturbed by your caring role?

- Is your health being affected? If so, how?

- Are you able to go out without worrying about the safety of the person you care for?

- Do you have any time for yourself?

- Are any of your other relationships being affected?

- Do you need information about benefits or other support available?

- Is your caring role having an impact on your job?

- How many hours per week are you caring, including the night times?

- What equipment is needed by the cared-for person to enable you to care for him safely?

- Do you have a wish to work, or remain in work?

- Do you want to pursue training or education activities?

It may be helpful to keep a diary recording some of the above, so that you can raise points during the assessment. During the carer's assessment, try to provide as much information as you can about how caring has affected you. It is important that all your needs are considered. If you do not feel that your assessment was adequate, or your circumstances have changed since you had an assessment, you can ask for a reassessment. The assessment will be used to decide what help, if any, can be provided for you by social services.

The introduction of the Carers (Equal Opportunities) Act 2004 in April 2005 means that in England and Wales there are some aspects of a carer's life which must be taken into account during the assessment. (This legislation does not apply in Scotland where an assessment of the carer's needs will only be carried out if the cared-for person receives social care services.) These considerations include whether the carer works or wishes to work and whether the carer wants to pursue education, learning and leisure activities. If these points are not addressed in your assessment, you should ask your social worker about them.

The results of the assessment should be recorded in a care plan. A copy of your written care plan should be given to you. This document is a written statement of your needs as a carer in your own right, detailing what support is necessary for you so that you can continue caring. These services should be in addition to any support services provided to the cared-for person by the local council's social services.

Delays in assessment

There is no time limit for how quickly a carer's assessment should be carried out. How long you wait will depend on the urgency of your situation. However, the social services department should complete an assessment within a 'reasonable' time. Many social services departments will have their own internal targets for providing assessments. These may be included in the customer charter or long-term care charter that is available from social services.

If you feel that the need for an assessment is urgent (e.g. the person you care for has become acutely unwell and you feel that you may need more help), an 'emergency' assessment by a duty social worker can be arranged for both you and the person you care for, if it is decided that the person you care for does not need to go into hospital for treatment. Social services may then arrange a temporary care package until a full care plan can be arranged. The person you care for may also be entitled to intermediate care – a free package of care provided for up to six weeks. This package is designed so that if the cared-for person needs a short-term stay in hospital or a care home for medical reasons, that stay is paid for by the local Primary Care Trust. Intermediate care packages can last for up to six weeks. If any equipment is needed by the person receiving intermediate care, this should also be provided free of charge. Intermediate care is available in someone's own home, in a care home, or in a community hospital. You should contact the older person's GP if you think that this may be needed.

Your right to request flexible working

In April 2006 it became a legal entitlement to request flexible working if you are a carer, so that you can fit your employment around your caring responsibilities. The government introduced this legislation to make it easier for carers to remain in work, because evidence shows that people who remain in work are much less likely to become poor or become socially isolated.

Your employer has a responsibility to consider this request for flexible working seriously. He is allowed to turn down the request, but he must provide evidence that there is a business case for doing so. Unless there is a business case, your employer should grant your request. The exact nature of your flexible working can be worked out on an individual basis with your employer, but may include working from home on particular days each week, starting work later in the morning and finishing later in the afternoon so that you can visit the older person before work, etc. It may also make things easier if you want to take time off work for emergencies, or to take the older person to have a hospital appointment, for instance.

The Work and Families Act 2006 covers those people who are a near relative of the person they are caring for, but does not apply to those people caring for a friend or neighbour. However, you may find that your employer will consider your proposals for flexible working kindly, even if you are caring for a friend rather than a relative. Your employer will benefit by being able to keep you in employment.

Support services available to carers

The assessment carried out by social services should help you identify what your needs, as a carer, are. During this assessment, the social worker should be able to tell you what services are available locally which are able to meet your needs. If your needs are to be met by the social services department, it will put in place these services for you. It may be that the needs you have cannot be met by services from the social services department, either because your assessed need is not high enough or because the department does not arrange such services. If this is the case, social services should still be able to signpost you to organisations in your local area which provide support services to carers. It may be that you can arrange care or support with these services privately.

These are the types of service which may be available to carers:

- Respite care to give you a break; for example, a sit-in service to enable you to go out, day care for the cared-for person, or a short-term placement in a care home or other setting away from his home

- Emotional support from other carers or people who understand your situation by way of attending a local carers' group (some groups also provide sit-in services)

- Aids and equipment, which can help both you and the cared-for person

- Direct payments, so that you can purchase services directly (see page 82 for more information about this)

- Welfare benefits advice

- Activities for the person you care for

The services you receive as a result of your assessment may be provided by a private or voluntary agency commissioned (and paid for) by social services.

Being charged for support services

If social services decide that you, the carer, are eligible for support services, you will need to answer some questions about your financial situation. If you have the means, you may be asked to pay for all or part of the service that the social worker arranges for you, provided the care you receive is not related to intermediate care. (If you, or the older person, receive intermediate care after a stay in hospital, for example, the services and equipment should be provided free of charge.)

Each individual local council decides what its social services department will charge for the domiciliary care and community care services it provides, and how these charges will be collected. However, the government has issued guidance to local councils about how they should structure their charging policies. This guidance, known as *'Fairer Charging Policies for Home Care'*, states that for domiciliary care services charges must be 'reasonable' and must not cause financial hardship. For people over 60, their level of income should not go below the Pension Guarantee Credit amount (£119.05 per week for a single person, £181.70 per week for a couple), plus a 'buffer' of 25 per cent. Any disability benefits you receive as a carer should also be taken into account as part of your income when calculating what is reasonable for you to pay.

Direct payments for carers

The Direct Payments Scheme is available to you as a carer. A 'direct payment' is money provided by social services which allows you to purchase the services you are assessed as needing, instead of their being provided directly by social services. Direct payments give you the choice about how to meet your needs to enable you to continue in your caring role and so you can maintain your own health and well-being.

As a carer you cannot use a direct payment to purchase services to meet the assessed needs of the person you are caring for. The payment must only be used to meet your **own** needs; for example, to pay someone to sit with the cared-for person for three hours once a week so you can go shopping or meet up with friends. The cared-for person is also able to apply for direct payments if he is assessed as needing support. Direct payments are available as a payment once a week, once a month or, in some cases, as a fixed one-off sum of money. The social worker will make the exact arrangements, helping you, as the carer, to organise the direct payment.

Welfare benefits available to carers

As a carer you may be entitled to claim Carer's Allowance, as well as being provided with support services. Some of these benefits are quite complex, and there are rules which state that more than one type of benefit cannot be claimed at the same time. If you want to get advice on this, you should contact an advice agency, such as Counsel and Care, or your local Citizens Advice Bureau.

Qualifying for Carer's Allowance

Carer's Allowance is a non-contributory state benefit for carers. This means that you do not have to have made National Insurance contributions in order to receive the allowance. In order to qualify for Carer's Allowance, you must:

- Be aged 16 or over

- Be caring for someone for 35 hours or more a week

- Be caring for someone who receives Attendance Allowance at either rate or the middle or higher care component of the Disability Living Allowance or Constant Attendance Allowance of £52.70 or more paid in conjunction with an industrial, war or service pension

- Be a resident in the UK

- Have lived in the UK for 26 weeks at least during the past 12 months

- Have no immigration conditions on your stay in the UK (subject to specified exceptions)

You can backdate your claim for up to three months.

But you do not qualify for Carer's Allowance if you:

- Earn over £87 a week net (after tax, National Insurance contributions, half of any contribution you make towards an Occupational or Personal Pension) and after any allowable deductions; or

- Are already getting £48.65 a week or more from certain other social security benefits or pensions such as Incapacity Benefit, State Retirement Pension, Severe Disability Allowance or Widow's Pension. These are known as the overlapping benefit rules, and you cannot claim both.

Carer's Premium

It may be that if you are not eligible for Carer's Allowance to be paid to you because you receive other benefits which amount to more than £48.65 per week, you may be eligible to receive the Carer's Premium, which is worth £27.15 per week. Receiving Carer's Premium will increase your entitlement to receive other means-tested benefits such as Pension Credit, which acts as a passport to Council Tax Benefit and Housing Benefit, but other benefits you or the cared-for person receive may be affected as a result of your claim. For example, if the person you care for receives Severe Disability Premium, he will lose this benefit when you begin claiming Carer's Allowance.

The difference between an allowance and a premium

Allowance: Some people may be entitled to an allowance or benefit if they meet certain criteria; for example, Carer's Allowance (£48.65 per week) can be claimed by people who care for someone for 35 hours or more a week. Attendance Allowance is paid to people who need extra money because they have a disability.

Premium: This is an extra entitlement added to someone's means-tested benefit (such as Pension Guarantee Credit), which allows him to be paid a higher level of that particular benefit. For example, the Carer's Premium allows someone to be paid an additional amount of £27.15 a week on top of his other benefits. He receives this whether he is actually paid the Allowance (because his weekly income is below £48.65) or not (because his weekly income is above £48.65).

Is Carer's Allowance worth claiming?

Claiming Carer's Allowance can affect other benefits that you, or the person you care for, receive. It may be that the money lost is more than £48.65, in which case you are financially better off if you do not claim the allowance. You may want to contact Carers UK for more details about this (tel: 0808 808 7777; www.carersuk.org).

If the person you care for is entitled to Severe Disability Premium as part of his means-tested benefit, he will lose this premium when you receive your first payment of Carer's Allowance. This means that even though you will receive Carer's Premium, the person you care for would lose his Severe Disability Premium worth £48.45 a week.

If the State Pension or other benefits you currently receive are less than the amount of Carer's Allowance, you may be entitled to receive a reduced amount of Carer's Allowance, raising your total benefits to the level of Carer's Allowance.

You can receive help and more information about Carer's Allowance and Carer's Premium from the Carer's Allowance Unit. The Unit can also help you complete an application form for the benefit. It can be contacted on 01253 856 123 or you can email cau.customer-services@dwp.gsi.gov.uk.

When Carer's Allowance or Carer's Premium will cease

Carer's Allowance is payable for eight weeks after you cease caring for the cared-for person if:

- he does not require your services any more;
- you choose not to be a carer any more;
- the person enters hospital; or
- he dies.

If the cared-for person enters long-term residential care, the Carer's Allowance stops on the day the person enters the care home.

If you experience this, so that you lose your Carer's Allowance, you may be eligible to apply for Jobseeker's Allowance. You can claim this if you are under the age of 60 and are out of work.

If you are over 60, you may be eligible for Pension Guarantee Credit if you now have an income below £119.05 per week.

Pension Guarantee Credit and Carer's Allowance

If you are aged 60 or over, have a low income, and are entitled to Carer's Allowance, you may be eligible to receive Pension Guarantee Credit, either for the first time or at an increased rate. If you, or your partner, receive Carer's Allowance, or if payment of Carer's Allowance is prevented because your Retirement Pension or other benefits take your weekly income above

£48.65, the Carer's Premium of £27.15 is added to your 'Appropriate Amount'. (This is the level of income which the benefit rules state is your suitable weekly income. The amount which is regarded as an 'Appropriate Amount' depends on your individual situation, any disabilities you may have, and whether you are a war veteran. Formulas are used to calculate what your Appropriate Amount is.) If you and your partner satisfy the rules, £27.15 is added to the calculation for each of you. This may result in you and your partner being eligible to receive Pension Guarantee Credit for the first time or to receive a higher amount than previously.

When can I make a decision for the older person?

A common situation for a carer is to be caring for an older person who may be in the early stages of dementia or who might have some sort of confusion which affects his decision making, some or all of the time. If you are the carer in this situation, you need to read page 87 about the implications of the Mental Capacity Act 2005, Enduring Power of Attorney and Lasting Power of Attorney. All of these measures have been put in place to help people make decisions on behalf of individuals who lack capacity; the measures ensure that when a decision is made in these circumstances, the people who lack capacity are safe and well. These decisions can relate to care and welfare, or the finances of the older person, or both. You do not have to be a family member to be able to make decisions on behalf of someone you care for, but you will have to show that you are able to make decisions in that person's best interests.

Q What is dementia?

A Dementia is a condition in which parts of the brain die away. This can cause memory loss, confusion and anxiety. Dementia varies in its severity. Sometimes people can live with it for years at a relatively low level, but in other people severe symptoms can develop very quickly. The symptoms of dementia can be erratic, so that someone may be able to make a reasoned decision at times, but be very confused at other times. In its early stages, dementia can be worked around, and people can continue to live independently in their own home. There are assistive aids which can help someone to remain safe. People who have very severe dementia may need support in a care home which specifically cares for people with dementia. These care homes are designed so that they are easy to walk around, that are as familiar and homely as possible, and where people are allowed to wander freely and without distress.

As a carer for someone with dementia, you may find that you are asked to make decisions on behalf of this person. This could be in relation to his care, medical treatment and welfare, or his finances. There are several safeguards which are set down in law to protect the people who lack capacity, and also protect those people making decisions.

Q My mother has only slight dementia and can still make some decisions. How can I help her?

A The key element of the Mental Capacity Act here is that people should be assumed to have capacity to make a decision unless it is proven otherwise. The professional opinion of a psychiatrist or psychogeriatrician (this is a psychiatrist who specialises in the mental health needs of older people) should be sought if there is doubt about whether someone can make a decision or not. This means that, where possible, an individual should be supported to make a decision for himself, rather than have someone else decide for him. If your mother wants you to make a decision on her behalf, this is entirely possible, because she has given you permission to make this decision, and is aware of what this means.

Q What does the Mental Capacity Act 2005 do?

A The Act deals with the assessment of someone's capacity and regulates the decisions made by those for someone who lacks capacity.

- **Assessing lack of capacity:** The Act says that someone should be assumed to have the capacity to make a decision unless it is proven otherwise. Capacity is also regarded as 'decision specific'. This means that someone can be assessed as having the ability to make a decision about one particular issue, but not about others. It also means that as long as a person has capacity while he is making the decision, it does not matter if he is later unable to make the same decision. This takes into account the fact that someone with dementia could be lucid at times, but at other times be very confused.

- **Best interests:** All decisions made on behalf of another person should be in his best interests. This means that it should be taken into account what the person may have decided had he been able to make the decision himself. If someone has written down what his wishes are, these should be taken into account when the decision is made. Family members and carers also have the right to be consulted when a decision is made.

- **Lasting Power of Attorney (LPA):** The Act allows a person to appoint an attorney to act on his behalf if he should lose capacity in the future. This is like the current Enduring Power of Attorney (EPOA), but the Act also allows people to let an attorney make health and welfare decisions.

- **Court Appointed Deputies:** Deputies will be appointed by the Court of Protection to take decisions on welfare, healthcare and financial matters. A Deputy can be a member of someone's family.

- **Independent Mental Capacity Advocate (IMCA):** An IMCA is someone appointed to support a person who lacks capacity but has no family or close friends able to speak for him. An IMCA would be involved in a decision about his treatment, care and welfare.

- **Advance decisions to refuse treatment:** A person may make a decision in advance to refuse treatment if he should lose capacity in the future. The decision must be in writing, signed and witnessed. In addition, there must be an express statement that the decision stands 'even if life is at risk'.

- **A criminal offence:** The Act introduces a new criminal offence of ill treatment or neglect of a person who lacks capacity.

If you are currently a carer for a person who has mild dementia, you should consider arranging with him for a Lasting Power of Attorney to be created, which is a legal document which entitles you to make decisions on his behalf if he lacks capacity in the future. This could be important in this situation, as if the dementia gets worse, he may not be able to make decisions in the future.

A Lasting Power of Attorney should be made while the older person still has the capacity to make a decision about who he wants to make decisions for him in the future. Once a Lasting Power of Attorney has been arranged, you will be able to make financial decisions on his behalf, as well as care and welfare decisions. Lasting Power of Attorneys will come into force in October 2007.

You should seek advice from the Citizens Advice Bureau or a solicitor if you want to arrange to set up a Lasting Power of Attorney, because it is a legal document.

If you reach a point where the older person has severe dementia and can no longer make decisions about his finances, care and welfare, and has not arranged for anyone to have a Lasting Power of Attorney over his affairs, you will need to apply to the Court of Protection to become a Court Appointed Deputy. This will also come into force in October 2007 and replaces the current system of receivership.

What if I am reading this before October 2007?

Some parts of the Mental Capacity Act do not come into force until October 2007 and if you are reading this before this date, the system will not have changed. The situation is a little different currently, because if a person lacks capacity, it is not possible to make any care and welfare decisions on his behalf, as this can only be made by medical and care staff. However, you can arrange for a Power of Attorney (POA) or Enduring Power of Attorney (EPOA), which means that you can manage a person's financial affairs for him, whether or not he lacks mental capacity.

If you have Power of Attorney for the older person, you can access his bank account, make payments, withdraw money, and sign cheques on his behalf. A Power of Attorney can be granted if he still has capacity, but no longer wishes, to manage his financial affairs. This is often useful if he lives in a care home and he cannot very easily access the bank, etc.

An Enduring Power of Attorney gives you the power to manage the older person's financial affairs after his mental capacity has been lost. This may be due to dementia or another condition which affects the brain, such as a stroke. However, this must be arranged while the older person is still able to make the decision to appoint you, and it must be registered at the Court of Protection. Once mental capacity is lost, it is not possible for you to be granted Enduring Power of Attorney. In this situation, the Court of Protection will appoint a 'receiver' (usually a relative) and the Court will decide what the receiver can spend money on.

You can arrange an Enduring Power of Attorney without a solicitor, using Lawpack's *Power of Attorney Kit*, but it would be wise for you to consult one for legal advice. You should also consider seeking advice from a Citizens Advice Bureau or an advice agency, such as Counsel and Care (tel: 0845 300 7585; www.counselandcare.org.uk), if you are thinking about setting one up.

Organisations which can provide further help to carers

The **Benefit Enquiry Line** is a national advice line run by the government which gives details about all the benefits available to older people, and their carers.

The **Carer's Allowance Unit** is the department which can give specific advice about claiming Carer's Allowance. It can also answer any questions about the overlapping benefit rules, which can make Carer's Allowance seem very complex.

Carers UK is a national charity which supports carers through information and advice, and it also campaigns on issues which affect carers. The organisation can help you find support groups and other resources in your local area.

Counsel and Care operates a national advice service for people over 60, their families and carers. The advice workers can assist with a range of issues, including the support available to older people, what do to if you are a carer, applying for benefits, and they can signpost you to local organisations.

The Princess Royal Trust for Carers provides care services across the UK through care centres. You can access services directly through the Trust or through your social services department.

The **Public Guardianship Office** is the administrative arm of the Court of Protection which is responsible for ensuring that attorneys or receivers are appointed to look after the financial affairs of people who do not have mental capacity. It registers Power of Attorneys and Enduring Power of Attorneys. In October 2007 the Office of the Public Guardian will take over this role.

CHAPTER 6

Caring for someone with dementia

THIS CHAPTER COVERS THE FOLLOWING:

- What is depression?
- Treatments for depression
- Loneliness leading to feelings of depression
- What is dementia?
- The symptoms of dementia
- Diagnosing dementia
- Making decisions for someone who has dementia
- Managing the finances of an older person with dementia
- Finding support services for someone with dementia
- Financial help and benefits available for someone with dementia
- Arranging health support for someone with dementia
- Support from the voluntary sector for people with dementia and their carers
- Caring for someone with dementia
- Financial help for carers
- Communicating with someone who has dementia
- Practical tips when caring for someone with dementia

- The behaviour of someone with dementia
- Finding accommodation for someone with dementia
- NHS continuing healthcare funding

Dementia can affect us all at any time of our lives, but people over 80 have a greater chance of developing the condition. According to the Alzheimer's Society, dementia affects 20 per cent of people over 80 years of age.

Dementia can affect people in different ways. Some people experience symptoms which are quite aggressive and develop in severity quickly, while others live with a mild form of dementia for many years and can still live independently in their own home.

It can be very distressing if an older person develops dementia. Because the disease attacks the brain cells, memory can be lost, and sometimes the older person forgets familiar faces or how to do straightforward tasks. If you are thinking about what care is available for an older relative, neighbour or friend who has developed dementia, this chapter will explain what services are available, and how you should make arrangements for them to be put in place. It also explains the rights of the person with dementia to retain as much control over his own decisions as possible.

Depression is also a mental health condition which often affects older people, and which is under-diagnosed in this age group. Symptoms of depression can sometimes be mistaken in older people, and they are considered to have dementia, or consistent low mood in older people is regarded as something inevitable, and so it remains untreated. This chapter begins by looking at depression and how it affects older people, before moving on to dementia.

What is depression?

Depression can affect anyone and can make someone feel low, empty and unable to cope or, in extreme cases, suicidal. Depression affects people in different ways. Symptoms may include:

- Ongoing sadness or feeling low
- Feelings of worthlessness, low self-esteem or low self-confidence

- Tearfulness

- Not sleeping at night

- Waking very early in the morning

- Poor concentration

- Poor memory

- Problems with eating

- Feeling anxious and worried

- Not wanting to go out or join in with social activities

Although it is not always recognised, depression affects older people just as much as younger people. This may be due in part to older people having to deal with bereavement or perhaps retirement and loss of social networks. Older people may also have to deal with health and mobility problems which could result in their becoming isolated and lonely.

Sometimes the symptoms of severe depression are mistaken for dementia. If a person has dementia, it may also make him feel depressed. This is why a comprehensive assessment from a social worker is needed as soon as possible to establish the underlying cause of the symptoms, which should include a health assessment. If the older person is showing symptoms of depression or dementia, you should arrange for him to see his GP, and also contact your local council's social services department for an assessment of need. There are lots of details in Chapter 2 of this guide about what an assessment of need is, who to contact to arrange one, and what happens during the assessment.

Treatments for depression

If an older person is diagnosed by his GP or by a psychogeriatrician (a specialist in the mental health needs of older people) as having depression, there are a number of treatments he could explore to help combat his symptoms. As a carer you could suggest the following treatments, or help the older person contact his GP to be referred to these services.

Counselling and support groups

Counselling gives someone the opportunity to talk freely and in confidence to a person who is not a friend or relative. The counsellor is trained to listen to the individual. Counselling can help the older person become more aware of why he is feeling the way he is, and help him to begin to feel more satisfied with his life.

There are many different types of counsellors. If the older person is considering counselling, it is important to find one that he feels comfortable with. Counselling can be conducted over the telephone or face-to-face. It can be a 'one-off' session, or regular meetings over a period of a few weeks or several months.

Self-help support groups also can give the older person an opportunity to talk with others who are feeling the same way or going through similar problems.

Counselling through the NHS

If you feel that counselling may help the older person, his GP may be able to refer him to a counselling service. Although counselling is not available everywhere, many GP practices employ counsellors. Some GPs may not mention counselling but you can ask them to make a referral. If they do not provide counselling through the Primary Care Trust, they should be able to signpost the older person to private or voluntary organisations who provide counselling in their local area.

Counselling through voluntary organisations

Some voluntary organisations offer counselling for specific problems, such as bereavement. Try your local library, GP notice board, a local Age Concern or Mind Association for such organisations in your area. (Their details will also be available in your local telephone directory.) You can contact them on behalf of the older person if he wants your help finding a suitable counsellor.

Private counselling

Another option, if affordable, is to see a private counsellor. Details of individual counsellors are available from the British Association for Counselling and Psychotherapy (tel: 0870 443 5252; www.bacp.co.uk). It is important that the counsellor is qualified and registered with BACP.

Psychotherapy

If the older person is diagnosed with severe depression, he may be referred to a psychologist or psychiatrist who will be able to provide him with more intensive therapy.

Medication for depression

Sometimes depression can be caused or aggravated by an imbalance of chemicals in the brain. Anti-depressant medication could help to correct the imbalance.

Anti-depressants can only be prescribed by a GP and they may need to be taken for six months or longer to treat the depression properly. There can be side effects from taking anti-depressant medication; for example, they may make someone feel sick, or more agitated. If this happens, contact the older person's GP promptly for his advice.

Loneliness leading to feelings of depression

Because many older people live alone and can sometimes find it difficult to meet other people, they may start to feel lonely. This can be difficult for you, particularly if you live some distance away from the older person, or you work long hours and find it difficult to see him. However, you can make some suggestions of ways to combat this:

- Contacting the older person's social services department could be a good place to start. The social services have a responsibility to assess anyone who contacts the department who it appears may be in need of care services. Some services the local council provides can help older people reduce their social isolation; for example, social clubs and day centres. You should request a care needs assessment which will establish what the older person's care needs are. The assessment should cover all of his care needs including his social, emotional and psychological needs.

- Contact the local library or Age Concern to find out what voluntary social clubs are available in the area where the older person lives. Dial-a-Ride and community transport schemes can be used to get to clubs. This can help him meet new people and get out of the house.

- Contact the older person's local Age Concern group for details of local befriending schemes, where trained volunteers visit the older person in his own home. Its details will be available in the local library or on the internet. Age Concern may run a befriending scheme or it could give details of other schemes in the local area.

- Contact the Elderly (tel: 0800 716 543; www.contact-the-elderly.org) is a voluntary organisation which organises Sunday outings for older people who are isolated.

- The older person could also think about offering a home to an unwanted pet for companionship. The RSPCA and local pet rescue organisations may be able to help someone choose a suitable pet. The Cinnamon Trust (tel: 01736 757 900; www.cinnamon.org.uk) and the Pet Fostering Service in Scotland (tel: 01877 331 496; www.pfss. org.uk) run schemes where pets are fostered if someone needs to go into hospital.

What is dementia?

The term dementia is used to describe conditions that cause the progressive loss of mental ability. Dementia will often affect the ability to remember, learn, think and reason. It may also cause a gradual loss of social skills.

Sometimes the symptoms of dementia develop slowly and the start of the condition is difficult to pinpoint. In other cases, dementia can develop suddenly and progress quickly. In either case, the effect on the person with dementia, his family and carers can be very distressing.

Dementia can affect people at any age but it is more likely to happen the older someone becomes. At the moment no one knows what causes dementia, and there is no cure, although treatments and medication are available and they can help to slow down the development of the disease.

It is important to remember that dementia is not an inevitable result of old age and that most older people will never suffer from any type of dementia. If you know a person who has been given a diagnosis of dementia which you do not agree with, you should make sure that you talk to his GP and understand the reasons for this diagnosis.

There are many different types of dementia, but the most common ones and their symptoms are listed below:

- **Alzheimer's disease:** This is the most common type of dementia. Alzheimer's disease is a physical disease, which causes a progressive decline in mental ability. The disease prevents certain brain cells from working normally. The causes of Alzheimer's disease are not fully understood and are still being researched. It is likely that a combination of factors, including age, genetics, diet and overall general health, affect whether someone gets the disease.

  The symptoms of Alzheimer's vary from one person to another. It often starts with the person becoming more forgetful and repeating himself. He might become worried about change and be unable to make decisions. He may also become more irritable and easily upset. As the disease progresses, his short-term memory may deteriorate and he may become confused about times and places. He might also start to lose his ability to understand other people and to make other people understand him. His personality may appear to change; he may resist assistance or behave in an unusual way. He may not be able to carry out basic living tasks, such as washing and dressing, and he may become dependent on someone else for his care needs.

  There are treatments available for Alzheimer's disease. Currently, some treatments are not prescribed on the NHS for people who have mild to moderate symptoms of Alzheimer's disease. The Alzheimer's Society has appealed against this decision, and the matter is currently the subject of a Judicial Review. Despite this, you should raise the possibility of obtaining treatment with the older person's GP. The Alzheimer's Society (tel: 0845 300 0336; www.alzheimers.org.uk) can offer information about these treatments.

- **Vascular dementia:** The next most common type of dementia is vascular dementia, which accounts for approximately 20 per cent of dementia cases. It is caused by damage to the blood vessels that carry oxygen to the brain, and it is usually triggered by either a major stroke or a series of smaller ones (referred to as 'multi-infarct dementia'). It is more common in people with a history of problems with their circulation or high blood pressure. Multi-infarct dementia usually leaves some of the brain's abilities intact. While there is no way to repair the damage already done to the brain, medical treatments may slow down or prevent the development of further symptoms.

- **Dementia with Lewy bodies (DLB):** People who have DLB will show symptoms usually associated with Alzheimer's disease. However, they may have major fluctuations in their abilities, sometimes on a daily basis. They will also typically suffer from symptoms usually associated with Parkinson's disease (stiffness, tremors and slow movements) and experience hallucinations. Diagnosis of DLB is difficult and people are often diagnosed as having Alzheimer's disease or vascular dementia.

- **Other forms of dementia:** There are rarer cases of dementia caused by a variety of other things: other degenerative brain diseases, damage to specific parts of the brain, alcoholism, HIV, or head injury.

The symptoms of dementia

Dementia usually develops over a long period of time, and not everyone will be affected in the same way. Some people may experience a rapid decline in their mental ability. However, dementia caused by Alzheimer's disease can take ten to 15 years to develop and may only become apparent if the person experiences a trauma, such as moving home, or a bereavement. A distinctive characteristic of vascular dementia is its 'step-wise' progression. This means that the symptoms are not gradual, but increase in a series of sudden changes. Some of the symptoms of dementia may demonstrate themselves in the following ways:

- **Learning:** The ability to learn new skills can be affected; for example, difficulties with learning how to use a microwave, or a new piece of equipment.

- **Memory:** Many people become more forgetful, particularly about the recent past; for example, whether they have taken their medication or not.

- **Communication:** Speech is often affected. People experiencing dementia may find it difficult to express what they want or to understand other people. This may cause feelings of frustration.

- **Personality and behaviour:** Many people experience significant swings in their emotions; for example, they may become suddenly tearful or angry. Other people may become withdrawn or believe that things are happening which are not. Others may walk around but forget their purpose (sometimes called 'wandering'). They may forget faces and names, even of familiar people. Others may experience very few personality changes or emotional difficulties.

- **Disorientation:** Some people find that they have a problem understanding times and places. Because of this, they may get lost or do things at an inappropriate time.

- **Depression:** This can affect people's ability to concentrate and cope with life.

- **Personal care:** Many people with severe dementia find it difficult to complete tasks in the correct order. They may need assistance preparing meals, washing, dressing and going to the toilet.

- **Judgement:** As the dementia progresses, people's ability to make judgements about the risks to themselves from hazards may diminish. For instance, they may not be able to use the cooker safely but are unaware of this.

- **Mobility:** As the illness progresses people's ability to keep their balance and walk steadily may deteriorate.

- **Continence:** Although lack of continence may be caused by a number of reasons, people with dementia may experience problems with continence because they may not recognise the need to use the toilet. If they have difficulty learning new skills and remembering learnt skills, they may not be able to locate the toilet. This issue is particularly important for people with dementia who are moving into a care home.

Many people who are in the early stages of dementia will only experience slight forgetfulness, mood swings and occasional out-of-character behaviour. People with advanced dementia are often severely affected and may require 24-hour care.

Diagnosing dementia

If you are worried that someone you know may have dementia, speak to the GP as soon as possible. He will be able to check whether the person you are concerned about is demonstrating signs of dementia and he will investigate the cause of the symptoms. Sometimes the symptoms are caused by other treatable conditions, such as depression, thyroid gland disorders or a reaction to certain drugs. It is very important that the possible other causes are investigated.

The GP will normally refer the older person to visit a psychiatrist who specialises in the care of older people for a full diagnosis – a psychogeriatrician. The older person may also be referred to a Memory Clinic, where professionals from a wide range of specialties will carry out thorough investigations to demonstrate the most likely cause of memory loss, and can therefore begin treatment. In order to be clear about the diagnosis, the psychiatrist may ask the older person to visit the assessment unit over the course of a few weeks. Also, a Community Psychiatric Nurse (CPN) may visit the older person at home.

More specialist advice about dementia can be obtained from the Alzheimer's Society (tel: 0845 300 0336; www.alzheimers.org.uk).

Making decisions for someone who has dementia

If you know an older person with dementia, you may find that you need to make some decisions on his behalf, if he is unable to decide for himself, or communicate his decision. There are rules in place to protect the person with dementia, as well as the person making decisions, and guidelines for the appropriate way to make these decisions. These rules are set out in the Mental Capacity Act 2005, which comes into force in stages during 2007. Family members and professionals who need to make a decision for someone who has dementia will have to comply with this legislation. Guides have been issued by central government for professionals, families and advisers on how the Mental Capacity Act should be followed.

The Mental Capacity Act 2005 starts with the assumption that everyone has, what is called, 'capacity' (the ability to make informed decisions), unless it is proven otherwise. The decision about someone's level of capacity is made by a psychiatrist, and it should take into account the individual circumstances of the situation. Someone may have the capacity to make some decisions but not others. From April 2007, the Mental Capacity Act creates Independent Mental Capacity Advocates, who help people to make important decisions when there are no family or friends to help them.

The Mental Capacity Act also sets into place some key principles which should be used if you need to make a decision on behalf of someone with dementia.

The Act creates a new role of Lasting Power of Attorney (LPA), which is a legal power given to someone to make health and welfare decisions, as well as financial decisions, for someone who lacks capacity. In a case where a person has lost capacity but does not have someone who has been nominated to have LPA, Court Appointed Deputies can take decisions about the same things. The Act also creates the principle of being able to make decisions in advance using 'advance directives', in which people can choose to refuse future medical treatment. But the decision about what health treatment is appropriate and available continues to remain with the health professionals. The person nominating an LPA should do so when he still has capacity. This should be someone that he feels he can trust to make decisions in his best interests in the future when he is no longer able to do so himself.

The role of Lasting Power of Attorney will be formally created in October 2007. Until then someone can have Enduring Power of Attorney, which involves a third party making financial decisions on behalf of someone who has dementia. Currently, no one other than the health professionals can make treatment decisions on behalf of someone with dementia. If a person currently holds an Enduring Power of Attorney, this will continue to remain as such after October 2007 and will not automatically change to the status of a Lasting Power of Attorney.

In Scotland, it is the Adults with Incapacity (Scotland) Act 2000 which covers these issues. For more information about this, you should contact Alzheimer's Scotland (tel: 0808 808 3000; www.alzscot.org).

Managing the finances of an older person with dementia

It is possible to make arrangements for a member of a person's family, or any other representative, to handle the financial affairs of someone who lacks mental capacity, whether or not he has dementia. If the older person does not lack mental capacity, this means that you can be granted Power of Attorney. You can have access to his bank account, can make payments, withdraw money, and sign cheques on his behalf. If the older person is losing the capacity to make financial decisions for himself, it is possible to apply for an Enduring Power of Attorney. This must be arranged while the older person still has capacity to make the decision. You may wish to seek advice from a solicitor about this legal document.

An Enduring Power of Attorney will need to be registered with the Court of Protection, and the solicitor will be able to assist you with this. An Enduring Power of Attorney will be replaced in October 2007 when a Lasting Power of Attorney can be given. A Power of Attorney will continue to exist as it does presently. Contact the local Citizens Advice Bureau or Solicitors for the Elderly (tel: 01992 471 568; www.solicitorsfortheelderly.com) to find a solicitor who can organise this.

If the older person is unable to make decisions and there is no Enduring Power of Attorney, someone will have to apply to the Court of Protection, who will appoint a 'receiver' (usually a relative) and decide what the 'receiver' can spend money on. An Enduring Power of Attorney can only be arranged when the older person is thought to have the mental capacity to make this decision. For details of the Court of Protection, contact the Public Guardianship Office (tel: 020 7664 7000; www.guardianship.gov.uk).

Finding support services for someone with dementia

Caring for someone with dementia can be difficult and at times stressful, but there are support services which you can arrange for the older person, in order to reduce the worry for him, and some of the caring burden which may fall on the family.

The first place to contact should be the social services department at the local council of the older person. The council has a duty to carry out a community care assessment if it appears that the older person may need its services. An assessment should look at all of the older person's care needs, as well as any difficulties caused by mental health. The council should look at housing needs, cultural or religious needs and psychological and emotional needs. Completing this assessment should mean that the specific needs of the older person are qualified and written into a care plan. This explains the type of help the older person needs and the services that are available to meet these needs. You can find more about the services available in Chapter 1 of this guide.

Q My mother only really needs some low level help a couple of times a week at the moment; where can I find this locally?

A Low level services are very difficult to find through social services departments, because they have recently had to cut back services so that they support only high level needs. If you are looking for services such as cleaning, shopping and collecting a pension, you can contact a local home care agency, who will be able to provide a carer to visit and undertake some of these smaller jobs. Talk to people in the local area to see if they can recommend a good agency. You can also contact the United Kingdom Home Care Association (UKHCA), which can give you details of agencies in a local area (tel: 020 8288 1551).

Financial help and benefits available for someone with dementia

People with dementia are particularly vulnerable when it comes to managing their money and they may need practical support with this. They may also have extra expenses, such as paying for care. You can apply for benefits on behalf of the older person, and there is a section on the application forms where you declare that it has been filled out on behalf of the claimant. It is important that the older person claims all of the benefits that he is eligible for, as this means that paying for care and support may become an option.

Attendance Allowance is a very important benefit for people with dementia. It is paid to people aged 65 and over, who are in need of care or supervision, and this can be as a result of physical or mental health support needs. It is not a means-tested benefit; it is determined solely by the care needs of the individual.

A person with mild dementia may qualify if he is becoming forgetful. He could become a danger to himself by leaving the gas on or the front door open and therefore would need supervision. However, he does not actually have to be receiving supervision or care to claim this benefit.

If the older person claims Attendance Allowance, he may also become eligible for Council Tax Benefit and Housing Benefit. Council Tax Benefit reduces the level of Council Tax that someone has to pay, and Housing Benefit is available to people who live in privately rented accommodation. Eligibility criteria have to be met before benefits can be awarded.

For more information about how to apply on behalf of an older person and for more details about Council Tax Benefit and Housing Benefit, you can call the Benefit Enquiry Line, which is run by the Department for Work and Pensions (tel: 0800 882 200).

Collecting the benefits

Benefits are paid into a nominated bank or building society account, and it is possible for you to collect them on behalf of an older friend or relative. The bank or building society can arrange this.

The Department for Work and Pensions can appoint someone to claim, receive and spend money on behalf of a person who is receiving benefits and is considered to be unable to handle his own financial affairs. You can get further information about appointees from the Benefit Enquiry Line number listed on page 106. Being an appointee will only allow you to deal with the receipt of benefits.

Arranging health support for someone with dementia

If possible, try to encourage the older person to contact his GP to see what services and support the GP is able to offer. This may be difficult, as recognising that there is a problem is uncomfortable to confront. You could offer to go along to the appointment with him, if this helps.

If someone is experiencing the symptoms of dementia, the GP should refer him to the local hospital's psychiatrist for older people, or the Memory Clinic, if there is one in the local area. A Memory Clinic is a special service which helps people who have dementia or memory problems to cope with their memory loss and to maintain or regain their daily life skills if these are affected by their memory loss. The psychiatrist will be able to make a more detailed diagnosis and establish if the symptoms are being caused by dementia. He will also provide advice on medication that may help to control the condition or slow down the development of the disease. Other health support services can also include:

- A **Community Psychiatric Nurse (CPN)** to give advice and support.

- **Day hospitals:** A person with severe dementia may be offered a regular place in a day hospital where he can receive nursing care and therapy as well as lunch and leisure activities. This support can help the carer also, by giving him a regular break from his caring role.

- **Respite care:** This is care received every now and then, for perhaps a couple of weeks at a time, in a hospital or care home. It allows batteries to be recharged for the person with dementia, and for the carer, giving him some important time off.

- **District nurses:** District nurses will visit a person in his own home to provide nursing care, such as changing dressings or giving medication.

- **Long-term NHS care:** If someone has severe dementia, he may be entitled to NHS continuing healthcare in either a hospital, a nursing home or your own home paid for by the NHS. Each Strategic Health Authority, the government body responsible for local healthcare, has its own rules for who can receive fully, or partly, funded continuing care by the NHS. You can ask your local Primary Care Trust for details of its eligibility criteria for this care (see your local telephone directory or the NHS website at www.nhs.uk).

Q I have heard in the news recently about medication for dementia being cut, is this correct?

A Yes, recently the National Institute for Clinical Excellence (NICE) has published guidance which is given to all local Primary Care Trusts (PCTs) in England and Wales. There is an equivalent body in Scotland called NHS Quality Improvement Scotland that regulates which drugs are available on the NHS in Scotland (www.nhshealth quality.org). These are the bodies which hold the purse strings for hospitals and GPs, and they give advice on which medications should be provided by the NHS. In the case of dementia medication, they have recommended that three treatments, Aricept, Exelon and Reminyl, which were previously used to treat mild to moderate dementia, should no longer be provided by PCTs. When a person's symptoms become more severe, he can then be prescribed the medication. NICE argued that the treatments were too expensive and did not provide value for money.

Critics have said that this is a bad decision, because many people have experienced the benefits that these drugs can offer. However, NICE has justified its guidance, saying that there are other forms of treatment which are equally effective. Anyone who is currently being prescribed the medication when the guidance was issued will continue to receive it. The Alzheimer's Society, and two related pharmaceutical companies, have filed for a Judicial Review of the decision in order to overturn it. At the time of writing, a final decision had not been reached.

Support from the voluntary sector for people with dementia and their carers

In many areas, voluntary and charitable organisations provide services to support people with dementia and their carers. A good starting point to find out about these services is to contact your local council's social services department or your local branch of the Alzheimer's Society.

Age Concern runs local groups and services, such as good neighbour schemes, lunch clubs and advice services. You can contact the national office to obtain details of your local group.

The **Alzheimer's Society** is a national organisation which supports people with dementia and those caring for them. It produces a wide range of booklets and fact sheets and it also has an information helpline. It has a network of branches throughout the country, which offer a range of services, such as advice and support groups.

Carers UK is a national organisation providing advice and support to carers. It also runs support groups where you can talk to people in similar circumstances. Social services or voluntary organisations, such as the Alzheimer's Society, may also run carers' groups.

The **Parkinson's Disease Society** provides advice and information to people who have Parkinson's disease, and their families and carers. It also can also give information about local support groups.

There may be other services provided by other voluntary groups depending on where you live. Your local library or council's social services should be able to tell you about these.

Caring for someone with dementia

It can be difficult to accept that someone you care about has dementia. It is also likely to be distressing to care for someone who is changing, especially if the person you care for no longer recognises people he is close to.

Although many carers find their role fulfilling, caring for someone with dementia can lead to feelings of anger, resentment, frustration and guilt. It may help to accept that these feelings will happen rather than trying to suppress them. There is, however, no easy solution to the problems and frustrations that carers face when dealing with complicated and distressing symptoms of an illness. Although the person with dementia may not be able to make sense of what is happening, he will still be able to sense atmosphere and tension.

Financial help for carers

If you care for someone with dementia for 35 hours or more per week, you may be able to claim Carer's Allowance (see Chapter 5 for further details).

Communicating with someone who has dementia

To make sure that you and the person you are looking after understand each other, it is important to check that any hearing aids, glasses or dentures are working properly. Speaking clearly and slowly to the person with dementia, rather than raising your voice, may enable him to understand and absorb what you are saying. You may have to repeat what you say, or he may find it easier if you write down what you want to say to him.

Your body language

Body language and touch can be very important in communicating with someone who has dementia, especially if he has difficulty understanding spoken communication. However, some people may feel threatened by this method. Again, it depends on the individual.

Past memories

Talking about the past can be a valuable experience for you as the carer and the person with dementia. Although dementia is responsible for memory loss, it is usually the short-term memory that is most severely affected. The person with dementia can normally remember some things from the past. Reminiscence therapy focuses on these memories. It can be comforting for both of you to talk about the past and share experiences.

Practical tips when caring for someone with dementia

Safety and hygiene

A person with dementia may forget to look after himself properly. It is important for the carer to help the person in a respectful, dignified and safe manner to manage tasks such as keeping clean and comfortable. It is important to make sure that:

- The bathroom is warm.

- There are non-slip rubber mats in the bathroom.

- There are grab rails on the side of the bath and toilet. (These can be bought cheaply from Disabled Living Foundation shops across the country. Telephone 0845 130 9177 for details of your local shop.)

- The cold water is run in the bath before the hot.

- Respect and dignity are offered at all times.

As hygiene is such a personal matter, it may be difficult for the carer to supervise or wash the person with dementia. For example, a daughter may find it difficult to have to bathe her father. If this is the case, contact your local council's social services to request an assessment of need and the possibility of a male home care worker to assist with bathing.

Dressing

Laying out clothes in the right order can make it easier for a person to dress himself. Some carers find that using slip-on shoes and easy fastening clothes (such as those with Velcro instead of small buttons) make dressing easier. It is also important for the person with dementia to choose the clothes that he likes to wear.

Eating

This can become a problem as a person with dementia can sometimes lose his appetite or find it difficult to use cutlery or to swallow. It will also be easier for him if the table is laid simply and there is just one set of cutlery on the table. You can buy specially designed cutlery, which makes eating easier (the Disabled Living Foundation (tel: 0845 130 9177; www.dlf. org.uk) has more information for you on what is available). The person will feel more settled and perhaps more secure if he eats at the same time every day.

If the older person appears to develop swallowing problems, contact his GP to request a referral for an assessment by a speech and language therapist. He can undertake an assessment and provide treatments to help with the swallowing problems.

Continence

Incontinence can also be a problem for someone with dementia. Seek advice from the older person's GP, remembering to ask whether the incontinence may be experienced as a result of a treatable medical condition. The GP should refer the older person to a specialist incontinence adviser in a local area. There are a number of aids available to help with this problem, such as Kylie sheets (one-way bed sheets) and incontinence pads (which are available from the NHS and can be sought through a GP). You might also want to contact the Continence Foundation, which has a helpline staffed by specialist nurses (tel: 0845 345 0165; www.continence-foundation.org.uk).

The behaviour of someone with dementia

'Wandering'

It is quite common for a person with dementia to be described as 'wandering'. This is when the person with dementia may be motivated to start something, but because of the effects of the dementia, there may be a breakdown in his ability to complete the task. The effect of this may cause the person with dementia to become agitated and distressed and he may appear restless. These symptoms can be worrying for a carer, especially if the person tries to leave his home. One reason for the behaviour may be the physical need for exercise, which may be alleviated by making sure that the person goes on regular accompanied walks or other forms of exercise. The Alzheimer's Society can offer advice on this subject.

'Aggressive' behaviour

Some people with dementia can present behaviour that appears aggressive. This is a symptom of the illness which is usually present for a set period of time and may appear or disappear at any stage of the illness. Aggressive behaviour is often the result of resistance to something they feel frightened about. As a carer, if you can identify what the person with dementia feels fearful about, you may be able to calm him. The psychiatrist or Community Psychiatric Nurse may also be able to give advice and help. You may find it helpful to discuss the issues at a carers' support group with other carers experiencing these difficulties. The Alzheimer's Society can provide details of local Alzheimer's groups and information on coping with aggressive behaviour.

Finding accommodation for someone with dementia

You may find that, despite your best efforts, you are unable to cope with the caring responsibility of looking after someone who has dementia. You should not feel guilty about this, and there are care and support options available to you and the older person. Clearly every effort should be made to ensure that the older person is as aware as possible of the changes that are needed, but he may not fully understand the implications of his situation.

Sheltered housing schemes

In some areas, sheltered or supported housing schemes have been developed which provide specialised help and care for people with dementia. For more information, contact the Elderly Accommodation Counsel (tel: 020 7820 1343; www.housingcare.org), or your local council's social services.

Care homes

There are care homes which are registered particularly to provide care for people who have dementia. Some care homes have a section within the home where they can look after people with these specific needs. You can obtain a list of care homes from the Elderly Accommodation Counsel (tel: 020 7820 1343; www.housingcare.org). You can also obtain inspection reports from the Commission for Social Care Inspection (tel: 0845 015 0120; www.csci.org.uk), and these may help you decide which homes to visit. The Alzheimer's Society can also provide a list of specialist care homes. Care homes registered for people with dementia may be described as EMI homes. This is an old term that stands for the Elderly Mentally Infirm.

If you are thinking about a move into a care home, you should contact the local social services of the older person to request a care needs assessment. More details about this can be found in Chapters 3 and 4 of this guide.

NHS continuing healthcare funding

The NHS can provide free continuing care funding. This can be provided in a hospital setting or a care home if the needs of the person with dementia are intense, complex, unpredictable, and require the input over a 24-hour period by a member of a multi-disciplinary medical team. However, a recent Health Service Ombudsman (HSO) report, known as the 'Pointon case', has established that this continuing healthcare can be provided in the person's own home if his symptoms of the dementia and behaviour meet the continuing care criteria of the local Strategic Health Authority.

It is important to recognise that mental health needs are just as important as physical care needs. Other HSO reports have stated that people with dementia are as entitled to continuing care funding as those with physical conditions. The number of continuing care beds is limited, and it can be quite hard to obtain the funding. If you think that the older person may be eligible for the funding, you should contact the psychogeriatrician or GP that is treating the older person.

Later in 2007 the Department of Health will publish a national set of continuing care criteria which should clarify the problems which have surrounded this funding.

CHAPTER 7

How to manage healthcare problems

THIS CHAPTER COVERS THE FOLLOWING:

- Healthcare in the community
- Occupational therapists
- Mobility problems
- Transport services
- Home Improvement Agencies (HIAs)
- Falls
- Keeping warm
- Continence issues
- Foot care
- Eye care
- Dental treatment
- Healthcare in hospital
- Planned admission to hospital
- Unplanned admission to hospital
- Finding care and support services after a discharge
- The welfare benefits available after a discharge from hospital
- Attendance Allowance and Disability Living Allowance

- Council Tax Benefit
- Housing Benefit

Many older people may find at some point that they need to obtain healthcare to treat a problem which they have developed. Some older people start to develop mobility problems, and age-related conditions, such as dementia or arthritis. It may be that this is affecting an older person that you know or care for, and you want to know how it can be treated, and who to contact.

Many older people also experience a hospital admission or hospital treatment at some point. This chapter explains what to expect if you know a person who is in hospital, and what to do about arranging for him to return home or receive support in his own home. It might be that he needs some respite care in a care home, or that he will no longer be able to live in his own home. We will look at the options available when a hospital discharge is being arranged.

Healthcare in the community

If the older person is experiencing problems with his health, you should advise him to seek advice from his GP in the first instance. This is the first port of call for any medical treatment or diagnosis needed.

The GP is part of the primary care service system of the NHS. These are the services which are often provided in the community, which also include dentists, community nursing teams, occupational therapists and physiotherapists. Healthcare provided by primary care teams is free at the point of delivery, apart from some one-off charges for prescriptions, eye tests, etc.

Occupational therapists

Occupational therapists are professionals trained to work with people who are ill or recovering from illnesses, or who have chronic disabilities. They can assist individuals to regain as much independence as possible. You may find that a social worker refers the older person to an occupational therapist for a needs assessment, or you can contact the therapist directly, or ask a GP to make a referral. Occupational therapists may be based in a hospital or other health setting, or in the social services department of a local council. If someone is in hospital, the occupational therapy assessment and subsequent provision of equipment should take place as part of the discharge process.

If the older person needs support or equipment after being discharged from hospital, any item of community care equipment up to the value of £1,000 and any intermediate care services that he is eligible for should be provided free of charge under intermediate care for a period of up to six weeks.

Mobility problems

Older people can experience a range of difficulties associated with older age and increased frailty. A common complaint is a reduction in mobility, and feeling stiff and sore. If this is affecting an older person you know, as well as seeking medical advice, he can obtain information about supportive aids and adaptations which are available to people in their own home. These are things like grab rails, ramps and gadgets to use in the kitchen which can help someone remain independent. These aids and adaptations are generally available to buy cheaply from Disabled Living Foundation shops (tel: 0845 130 9177; www.dlf.org.uk to find your nearest shop).

Transport services

It may be that the older person is unable to get out and about as easily as he used to. Disabled people may have difficulty with access to public transport, but in many areas there are community transport schemes, such as Dial-a-Ride. These organisations can provide door-to-door transport for older or disabled people. In some areas, there will be taxis or community buses that have disabled access. Contact the local council's social services department for more information about these. In some areas, there are volunteer schemes which can arrange transport with approved volunteers. Contact your local council, local Age Concern, Women's Royal Voluntary Service (WRVS) or Red Cross to see if this service is available. Sometimes local charity groups, such as the Multiple Sclerosis Society, have their own transport schemes.

If the older person drives a car, his social services department can arrange to provide him with a blue badge for his vehicle, provided that he has a disability. This enables him to park in more convenient locations.

Home Improvement Agencies (HIAs)

These not-for-profit agencies exist to assist older people, disabled people and low income home owners and private tenants to have repairs carried out, as well as adapting or improving their homes. They can advise on how to claim grants to help the older person raise money. Some HIAs can arrange for minor repairs and/or adaptations to be carried out at a subsidised rate by a member of their staff or an approved company. One of the major government grants to help with this kind of work is the Disabled Facilities Grant.

HIAs can come under many titles, but are often called 'Anchor Staying Put' (tel: 0191 270 6069; www.stayingput.org.uk) or 'Care and Repair' (tel: 0115 950 6500; www.careandrepair-england.org.uk). HIAs exist in about two-thirds of local councils and their contact details may be obtained from their national body, Foundations (tel: 01457 891 909; www.foundations.uk.com). If there is no HIA in the area near to the older person, you should contact his council or local advice centre directly to find out what help is available. If the older person is a council tenant, he should contact the council's housing department to notify it about a repair. If he rents his home privately, he should contact his landlord. The permission of the landlord will be needed before any repairs or adaptations can be carried out.

Falls

As people grow older, they may become more prone to falls. Falls can cause serious injury as reduced mobility can lead to muscle weakness. Amongst older people, a broken hip is the most common injury after a fall, and injuries sustained after a fall are the leading cause of death from injury in people over 75. However, many falls can be prevented by encouraging your the older person to take the following simple steps:

- **Staying active:** Falls can be caused by weak muscles and poor balance. Older people can improve their muscle tone by taking regular exercise, such as walking or doing light gardening and housework. You could also consider contacting the older person's local council's social services department to see if there is a 'healthy living centre' near where he lives. These centres often run keep-fit classes for those with restricted mobility or disability problems.

- **Reduce risk:** If the older person is experiencing difficulty with activities such as getting into or out of a chair, or going to the toilet, you can request an occupational therapist assessment from his local council's social services to establish if there is any equipment or adaptation which can assist him with this difficulty.

- **Awareness of health changes:** Highlight the benefits of regular eye check-ups. The older person may be entitled to a free NHS eye examination, and help with the cost of glasses. He may be able to have a home visit by an optician if he has problems getting out and about.

- **Medication:** If the older person is taking more than four different types of medication, his GP should review them on a regular basis.

- **The flu jab:** Everyone over 65 is entitled to have a free flu jab each year. GPs should contact eligible patients automatically, but if the older person has not been called for a jab, he can ring the surgery to arrange an appointment.

- **The importance of diet and fluids:** A balanced diet is important for older people, so that they can maintain their strength and bone density.

- **Reducing hazards:** Small changes to a home can help reduce accidents. Here are a few suggestions:

  - You could help the older person fit a letterbox cage so that he does not need to stoop to pick up letters.

  - Fit 60-watt energy-saving light bulbs in the kitchen and stairways to make it easier for the older person to see any potential hazards.

The energy-saving bulbs do not have to be changed as often; therefore, they reduce the need for him to climb on chairs or stepladders.

- Ask the older person if he has considered fitting handrails next to the toilet, bath, stairs and front door. These will help him with balance and can make moving around more safe.

- Check that frayed carpet edges are removed or repaired.

- Help the older person to store frequently used items somewhere easily accessible.

- Offer assistance with chores, such as changing curtains or light bulbs.

- Community alarm systems can provide reassurance if the older person is at risk of falling. They are operated on a pendant worn around the neck, and you can arrange for the alarm to contact you or another relative so that you can provide assistance, if needed.

To obtain further information about any of these suggestions, contact the local Age Concern, local social services department or Home Improvement Agency. All of them will accept enquiries from a friend or relative, but they will want to know that the older person is happy with any changes that take place. It is really important that while you feel you are protecting the older person, you do not 'take over' or dominate him while he is still able to make decisions for himself.

Keeping warm

The health of older people can often be adversely affected if they live in a cold home. If the older person requires assistance to help him with heating or insulation improvements, this can be obtained from Warm Front, which is a government scheme providing grants up to the value of £2,700, to qualifying households. The Warm Front Scheme (Warm Deal in Scotland, Home Energy Efficiency Scheme in Wales and Warm Home Grant in Northern Ireland) will assist households who either own or privately rent their homes and would benefit from the amendments, or where there is the greatest risk of the person suffering from lack of heating.

To be eligible, someone must be over 60 and in receipt of Pension Credit or disability benefits. You can call free on 0800 952 1555 to make an application and check the criteria on behalf of the older person.

There may also be grants, discounts or subsidised work offered through energy providers and local authorities for insulation and energy-efficiency work. The Home Heat Helpline (tel: 0800 33 66 99; www.homeheat helpline.org) offers advice on subjects including cheaper fuel payment schemes, grants for insulating homes, and how to register for extra services and government benefits. It can also give information about the priority services register, which vulnerable older people can be listed on. Being listed on this register means that people who would be most at risk if there was a loss of fuel supply are contacted in the case of an emergency.

Continence issues

It is estimated that six million adults in the UK currently experience some form of incontinence, but because it is a sensitive subject many health professionals estimate that there may be many other people who experience problems but do not receive assistance. It is important to remember that incontinence is not an inevitable result of growing older. However, certain age-related changes do occur in the nervous system, kidneys, bladder and urethra (the tube that carries urine from the bladder out of the body) which can make older people more vulnerable to developing incontinence.

There is a difference between the two main types of incontinence. One is physiological, caused because a person does not know when he needs to go to the toilet or because he cannot control his bladder or bowels because of a disease, disability or illness. The other is environmental, and may occur because someone is not able to get to a toilet in time as a result of mobility difficulties.

Making an appointment to see a GP if there are continence issues is very important, and he may well be able to refer someone to a continence nurse who can give specific advice about treatments for incontinence. It may be that there are exercises that the person can do in order to strengthen muscles around his bladder.

If there are environmental issues that mean someone is unable to get to the toilet in time, there are a number of aids and adaptations available to help make access easier. You can contact the occupational therapist at the social services department of the older person, the Disabled Living Foundation (tel: 0845 130 9177), Care and Repair (tel: 0115 950 6500) or other Home Improvement Agencies (contact Foundations to get local details – tel: 01457 891 909).

Sometimes people who have experienced physiological damage (e.g. caused by a stroke) may no longer be aware of when they need to go to the toilet. Loss of mental ability can also lead to people being unaware that they need to go to the toilet. If you realise that the person you are caring for may be having problems with incontinence because he lacks awareness, you should seek professional advice to find out if the symptoms are temporary or likely to be permanent. Seeking help at an early stage increases the chances of the problem being resolved or at least improved. You may find that by changing diet, daily routine, carrying out special exercises and drinking at different times of the day, it is easier to cope with incontinence.

For more information and advice about continence issues, you can contact the Continence Foundation (tel: 0845 345 0165; www.continence-foundation.org.uk), which operates an advice line and publishes fact sheets which can be downloaded from its website.

Foot care

Looking after the feet of older people can help with mobility problems and also reduce the risk of someone falling. Older feet tend to develop more problems because the skin is thinner and wear and tear on the joints over the years may be causing discomfort or pain. However, this is not a natural part of growing old, and there are treatments available which can improve the condition of someone's feet.

If the older person has problems with his feet because of ageing, diabetes, osteoarthritis or rheumatoid arthritis, he should be a priority for NHS foot care services. He should make an appointment to see his GP, and ask to be referred to a podiatrist or chiropodist.

If he is not eligible for foot care from the NHS, he will need to arrange to see a chiropodist privately. Some local older people support groups, such as Age Concern or Shopmobility, arrange group chiropody appointments. You may wish to check with the local agency to see if this service is arranged by them. It would be possible to make an appointment of behalf of the older person, if this is necessary.

Eye care

Many older people find that their eyesight degenerates a little in their old age, and that they need to start wearing glasses. It is therefore important that older people receive regular eye tests. They are entitled to a free eye test every two years if they are aged between 60 and 70, and every year if someone is over 70.

You can find opticians who undertake free eye tests on the NHS website (www.nhs.uk) or by contacting your local Primary Care Trust.

If the older person's sight test shows that he requires glasses, he will be provided with a prescription which he can take to any optician or supplier to have prepared. If he has a prescription which is defined as 'complex', or he receives Pension Guarantee Credit, he is also entitled to vouchers to assist with the cost of his glasses. (If his income is low, he can ask for a voucher when he has his eye test. He will be required to provide evidence that he qualifies for this.) You can check if he qualifies by obtaining Form HC1 from the Health Literature Line (tel: 0800 555 777). If he does qualify, he will be sent an HC2 or HC3 Certificate, which shows that he is eligible for help. If he needs help completing the form, voluntary agencies such as Age Concern (tel: 0845 600 2001; www.ageconcern.org.uk) may be able to assist you.

If the older person has a severe sight impairment (one that cannot be corrected by glasses), there is a government system in place that registers people who are blind or partially sighted. This registration of severe sight impairment (Certificate of Vision Impairment) will be used to notify the older person's local council's social services of his difficulties and trigger his need for a needs assessment. This means that social services will become aware of the older person's likely need for support as a result of his eyesight.

Dental treatment

Often older people find that they require services from a dentist, because they need dentures, or because they have other problems with their teeth. Free NHS treatment is provided for people who receive Pension Guarantee Credit, but partial help with dentist's costs may also be available.

In April 2006 there were new charges introduced for NHS dental care, designed to make the system simpler for those people who are not eligible for help with the charges. The maximum charge for a complex course of treatment is now £194, and other more straightforward treatments or check-ups now cost either £15.90 or £43.60.

If you want to find an NHS dentist, you can search on the NHS website (www.nhs.uk) or call your local Primary Care Trust (PCT), which should be able to tell you about the local dentists which are registering new NHS patients. You can find details of your PCT from the same website, or in your local telephone directory or library. If you are unable to find a dentist which accepts NHS patients, you may find that you have to pay privately for dental treatment.

Healthcare in hospital

There is currently an emphasis from the government and the Department of Health to provide more healthcare services in the community. This benefits older people because they are able to access the services more quickly, which are provided in one location. It also reduces the need for hospital admission, which can bring its own risks; for example, MRSA infection, etc. It is also less expensive for the health service, because in-patient care is much more intensive. For minor treatments and with the right levels of support in the community, people can receive treatment and go home the same day. There is also the added benefit that if problems are treated quickly before they get too serious, hospital admissions can be reduced or prevented altogether.

However, even with good community health services, there is sometimes still a need for hospital admission. This can be a difficult time for an older person and his family, and in many cases it requires a change of accommodation or support after the older person has been discharged.

If you are in the situation where the older person is in hospital receiving treatment and the staff are discussing discharge plans, you should ask them about these plans so that you know what to expect. Staff should be able to provide friends and relatives with a written discharge plan which you can read through. People in hospital have certain rights so that they are discharged safely and with the appropriate services in place. People should have all of the necessary assessments, should be informed about any changes in benefits, or which benefits they may now be eligible for, and under no circumstances should be discharged before the appropriate plans have been put in place.

> **Q** I have heard of delayed discharge fines. What does this mean for the older person in hospital?
>
> **A** Delayed discharges are a system of fines charged by hospitals against local councils. They operate when a patient is ready medically to be discharged from hospital because he no longer needs healthcare in that environment, but when the social services department has not undertaken its duty to ensure that there is appropriate accommodation or community services ready. This means that a person is 'bed blocking'; that is, he is preventing the use of a bed which could be used for another patient.
>
> The effect this can have is that the social services department is so keen to move the patient out of hospital to avoid a fine that the patient is not moved into appropriate accommodation. If this happens to the older person, and you are unhappy with the plans for accommodation and care after discharge, you should raise your concerns with the doctor in charge. Explain that you do not feel an appropriate discharge plan has been put in place, and tell him what you would like to be different. You should not accept a discharge plan that you are unhappy with.

Planned admission to hospital

If the admission to hospital has been planned in advance (e.g. an operation), you can help the older person to make arrangements in advance for his discharge. This will mean talking to the hospital doctor in charge of the older person's care before the operation to ask about probable timescales, and how quickly he may be allowed to leave hospital.

If the older person currently lives alone in his own home, you could consider respite care if it is likely that he will need a couple of weeks to regain his strength and recover from the treatment that he has received. The hospital will be able to advise which respite care centre is most suitable for the older person and, if respite care is needed, it will make the necessary arrangements. Respite care should be provided free of charge by the NHS for up to six weeks.

If the older person is able to move directly back into his own home, he could consider arranging for friends or neighbours to visit him, if he needs help with shopping, etc. There are also Home from Hospital schemes available in some areas, where volunteers will make sure that there is essential food in the house when the older person returns from hospital and that the heating has been turned on, etc. They will also visit the following day and week to make sure that the older person has settled well and has no problems. To find your nearest Home from Hospital scheme you can call Counsel and Care (tel: 0845 300 7585; www.counselandcare.org.uk) or your local Age Concern or other similar advice agency.

The discharge should be planned before the older person has even gone into hospital, and the staff should consider from the beginning of the treatment how they are going to manage the discharge, and they should ensure that the appropriate assessments have taken place.

Before the older person is discharged, he must have received an assessment from a social worker at the hospital, or a social worker in the community. This assessment will take into account any care or support needs he has and if the council is able to provide these services, it should ensure that they are put in place for the older person when he returns home.

Unplanned admission to hospital

Sometimes treatment in hospital is not planned and it occurs after a condition suddenly gets worse, or the person has a fall. In this situation it is obviously less easy for you, and the older person, to make plans. If you live close to the older person, you can arrange to visit him in hospital and reassure him that the house is safe and all the lights are turned off, etc. You may want to visit the house to check that everything is OK. If it was left in a hurry, for example, the windows may still be open, etc.

Planning for the discharge of the older person should start to take place as soon as he is admitted. Any ongoing treatment should be considered and, as with planned admissions, the necessary assessments and home support arrangements should be considered thoroughly before discharge goes ahead.

It may be that the hospital episode means that the older person cannot move back into his own home, at least not immediately. If you have to look for a care home, do not feel pressured into moving the older person into a home until you are happy with the arrangements.

Finding care and support services after a discharge

You can find local care and support services for the older person in a few ways. It is important to make sure that the older person has had a care needs assessment conducted by a social worker, so that you know what support services are required. It may be that the social services department can provide the services itself, in which case you may not need to arrange any further support.

However, if you want to arrange some additional support, or the older person is not eligible to receive social services' support, you have a number of options. If the older person will only need support for a couple of weeks, can it be arranged that a few family, friends and neighbours work together to provide some informal support with shopping, etc. for a short time? You could also consider word of mouth – does the older person know any friends in the area who receive home care services, or respite care somewhere? Try contacting people whom you have received good reports about.

If you need to arrange home care services, social services will be able to give you a list of approved agencies in the local area. You should contact the department to tell it that the older person has had a needs assessment, and explain what sort of support he requires. The manager of the agency will arrange to visit the older person in hospital before he returns home.

If care in a care home is needed, on either a temporary basis or a longer-term basis, again it is vital that a care needs assessment and a financial assessment have been carried out by a social worker. You should read Chapters 3 and 4 of this guide, which explain how to find a suitable care home and how it is funded.

The welfare benefits available after a discharge from hospital

The older person may become eligible for welfare benefits after he is discharged from hospital. Some are means tested, and are therefore dependent on the income and savings of the older person, and some are dependent on the physical condition of the older person and how much support he needs. If you need any further information about the benefits available to older people, you should call an advice agency such as Counsel and Care (tel: 0845 300 7585; www.counselandcare.org.uk) or the Benefit Enquiry Line (tel: 0800 882 200).

Attendance Allowance and Disability Living Allowance

Attendance Allowance (AA) and Disability Living Allowance (DLA) are non-means-tested benefits paid to people who have health problems or have a physical disability or mental health needs. Attendance Allowance is a benefit paid to people aged 65 and over who have care or supervision needs. In 2007–08 it is paid at a rate of £64.50 per week if you have high needs, and £43.15 if you have more moderate needs. Disability Living Allowance is a benefit paid to people aged under 65 who have care or supervision needs or who have difficulties with mobility. The rate of benefit received depends on the level of mobility and care needs of the individual. There are more details about these benefits in Chapter 8.

Council Tax Benefit

Council Tax Benefit reduces the Council Tax bill that someone receives. How much it is reduced by depends on the income of the individual, and can be up to a 100 per cent reduction, so no tax is charged. The older person will not have to pay Council Tax if he moves into a care home, but he will be liable for it in a sheltered or extra care housing scheme. Council Tax Benefit is administered by the local council. If someone receives Pension Guarantee Credit, he is entitled to full Council Tax Benefit and Housing Benefit.

Housing Benefit

This is paid by a person's local council if he is on a low income and is living in a rented property. People with savings below £16,000, as well as meeting other set criteria, will be eligible to receive the benefit. The amount of Housing Benefit received is based on what the council decides is an 'eligible rent'. This may not be the same amount as the actual rent paid for a property.

For further information about benefits, whether the older person may be eligible for them, and how to apply for the benefits, contact the Benefit Enquiry Line run by the Department for Work and Pensions (tel: 0800 882 200).

CHAPTER 8

The welfare benefits available to older people

THIS CHAPTER COVERS THE FOLLOWING:

- Pension Guarantee Credit
- Pension Savings Credit
- Attendance Allowance
- Housing Benefit
- Council Tax Benefit
- Disability Living Allowance
- Carer's Allowance
- Carer's Premium

Many older people are eligible for benefits, as a result of either their age or their condition. Some benefits can be claimed if a person has a particular health condition or a support need which is related to a health condition. Some benefits are affected by the National Insurance contributions individuals have made in their lifetime and other benefits cancel each other out. Some benefits have the same eligibility criteria so that if the older person is eligible for one, he is eligible for a group of benefits. Other benefits are assessed according to the savings and weekly income of the older person, and are available to those on the lowest income. Because of the complexity of the system it is possible that an older person you know may not be receiving all of the benefits he is entitled to receive.

This chapter sets out the main benefits which are claimed by older people. If you know someone who may not be claiming all of his benefits, or you want to check that the older person is maximising his income, you should read this chapter. The complex rules mean that this chapter contains general information only, but there are phone numbers listed throughout if you want more information about a particular benefit mentioned.

You can help the older person apply for all benefits by telephoning for forms on his behalf or helping him to fill out the necessary information on the forms themselves.

Pension Guarantee Credit

Pension Guarantee Credit is a means-tested benefit paid to people over 60 living in the UK. This means that a person can receive the benefit if his weekly income is below a set minimum amount, which in 2007–08 is £119.05 for an individual and £181.70 for couples. Broadly speaking, if a person's income is below this amount, Pension Guarantee Credit will top up his income to this level.

Qualifying income

The Department for Work and Pensions will assess a person's weekly income, which is called his 'qualifying income'. The main sources of qualifying income which are considered are:

- State Retirement Pension
- Private or occupational pension
- War Disablement and War Widower's Pension (the first £10 is disregarded)
- Assumed income from savings (£1 for every £500 above £6,000)
- Earnings
- Certain social security benefits

Disregarded income

Certain sources of income are ignored, which means that they are not taken into account in consideration of what is qualifying income:

- Attendance Allowance or Disability Living Allowance
- Housing Benefit and Council Tax Benefit
- Social Fund payments
- Voluntary and charitable payments
- War Widow's and Widower's Pension of £70.88 introduced in April 1990 for 'pre-1973 widows' (in addition to the £10)
- The first £5 of any weekly earnings
- The first £20 if the claimant is disabled or is a carer
- The first £10 of income from a War Widow's or Widower's Pension
- The first £10 income from a War Disablement Pension
- The first £20 income from a tenant
- Direct payments from social services for any personal care

The Department for Work and Pensions will assess the total income of the older person. If his income is below £119.05, he will receive a top-up of Pension Guarantee Credit until he reaches this amount.

The older person can apply for Pension Guarantee Credit by telephoning the Pension Credit Helpline (tel: 0800 991 234). The helpline advisers can fill out the form over the telephone, or they can post a written copy of the form to the older person if he prefers this. As a carer or relative, you can ring on someone else's behalf to request a form.

Pension Savings Credit

This is a benefit to reward people who have made modest savings over their lifetime. Only a person's qualifying income is rewarded. If the older person has income from a State Retirement Pension or private pension of between £87.30 and around £158 per week, and he is over 65, then he will be entitled to Pension Savings Credit. The maximum savings credit a single person can receive is £19.05 per week.

Someone can be eligible for Pension Savings Credit, but not eligible for Pension Guarantee Credit.

To find out more, or to claim Pensions Savings Credit, you can call the Pension Credit Helpline (tel: 0800 991 234). You can also use the Pension Credit calculator at www.direct.gov.uk.

Attendance Allowance

Attendance Allowance is a benefit for people over 65 who have some form of care and support needs, and who are living independently in their own home. It is designed to cover additional costs which may be related to someone's disability; for example, extra travel costs, heating bills, or paying for a carer or home help. Attendance Allowance can be claimed regardless of income and savings, as these are not taken into account. Only the care and support needs of the individual are taken into account in the decision to award the benefit.

To qualify for the benefit, someone needs to have required care and supervision for six months prior to making the claim. It can be claimed if the older person has problems with one or more of the following:

- Getting dressed or undressed
- Washing, shaving or cleaning his teeth
- Brushing or washing his hair
- Using the toilet or managing incontinence (such as buying or changing pads)
- Taking medication or receiving medical treatment
- Walking, standing or going upstairs
- Getting in or out of bed
- Sitting down or getting out of a chair
- Taking baths or showers

- Turning over or settling in bed
- Reading, cooking or getting around if he has sight problems

Or

- He is unsteady on his feet
- He may fall or have accidents
- He cannot see or hear very well
- He gets confused or forgetful
- He may have a seizure or dizzy turn
- He has an illness which comes on quickly
- He finds it difficult to control his behaviour
- He cannot be left alone

Attendance Allowance is paid at a lower rate of £41.65 per week, and the higher rate of £62.25. The higher rate is paid if someone needs care and supervision during the day and also at night.

Attendance Allowance can be claimed by calling the Benefit Enquiry Line (tel: 0800 882 200), by collecting Form AA1A from a local Post Office or downloading a copy from www.direct.gov.uk. There is also an Attendance Allowance Helpline (tel: 0845 712 3456), which can deal with any other queries you may have about this benefit.

Housing Benefit

Housing Benefit can be claimed if an older person pays rent, lives on a low income and has less than £16,000 in savings. He can rent his house from the local council, a social housing landlord or a private landlord. It is co-ordinated by local councils.

Housing Benefit will pay for what the local council considers to be eligible rent. This may be lower than the actual rent being paid by the individual. Eligible rent can depend on whether the rent paid is reasonable for the size of the home, whether the home is a reasonable size for the individual's needs, and whether the rent paid is reasonable for the local area.

Housing Benefit can also cover service charges, which are often incurred when someone lives in a rented property. Charges covered include:

- Fuel charges for heating in parts of the building that a person shares with other people, such as communal hallways or landings
- Charges for cleaning shared areas
- Furniture or equipment that has to be rented from the landlord
- The upkeep of the garden, lifts, entry phones and rubbish removal costs
- Some of the costs of a resident warden

The council will take into account the weekly income of the older person when it decides whether or not he is eligible for Housing Benefit. Income included in this consideration includes:

- Any earnings
- Some welfare benefits (although Attendance Allowance or Disability Living Allowance are ignored)
- Income from anyone living with the claimant; for example, a son or daughter
- Tax credits
- Occupational pensions
- The capital savings belonging to the claimant and his partner

You can contact the Benefit Enquiry Line (tel: 0800 882 200) to receive an application form, and you can phone on behalf of the older person if you think that he may be eligible.

Council Tax Benefit

Council Tax Benefit is administered in a similar way to Housing Benefit, and there are income and savings rules which are the same. It is likely that if the older person is eligible for Housing Benefit, he will also be eligible for Council Tax Benefit.

A person can claim Council Tax Benefit if:

- he has to pay Council Tax, has less than £16,000 in capital savings; and
- he is on a low income; or
- he lives with one other person who is not his partner and who is on a low income.

If a person receives Pension Guarantee Credit, there is no savings limit to his claim for Council Tax Benefit.

Council Tax Benefit is not worth a fixed amount – it depends on the income of the individual, how much help he receives towards his Council Tax bill and it can be up to 100 per cent of the bill.

Council Tax Benefit is co-ordinated by local authorities, but claims can be made by calling the Benefit Enquiry Line (tel: 0800 882 200). If you are calling on behalf of the older person about his Housing Benefit or Council Tax Benefit, you should enquire about both at the same time.

The Department for Work and Pensions should automatically refer everyone who applies for Housing Benefit, Council Tax Benefit or Attendance Allowance to each of these benefits, as the eligibility criteria are so similar. The telephone claim line should help the older person complete one application form for all three benefits.

A decision about the benefit should be made within 14 days of making the application. Council Tax Benefit, Housing Benefit and Attendance Allowance all stop four weeks after moving into a care home.

Disability Living Allowance

Disability Living Allowance is a benefit for people under the age of 65 if they have mobility difficulties. It is similar to Attendance Allowance, because it is a benefit which is designed to help people with additional costs related to a disability or care and support need. Once you have been awarded Disability Living Allowance it can be continued beyond the age of 65. To claim Disability Living Allowance, you need to have required help for three months and be likely to need the help for at least another six months, or have a terminal illness.

Disability Living Allowance is split into two components – the care component and the mobility component. The care component can be claimed if a person needs help with personal care or needs supervision by another person to prevent harm to himself or other people. For example:

- Getting dressed or undressed

- Washing, shaving or cleaning his teeth

- Brushing or washing his hair

- Using the toilet or managing incontinence (such as buying or changing pads)

- Taking medication or receiving medical treatment

- Walking, standing or going upstairs

- Getting in or out of bed

- Sitting down or getting out of a chair

- Taking baths or showers

- Turning over or settling in bed

- Reading, cooking or getting around if he has sight problems

Or

- He is unsteady on his feet

- He may fall or have accidents

- He cannot see or hear very well

- He gets confused or forgetful

- He may have a seizure or a dizzy turn

- He has an illness which comes on quickly

- He finds it difficult to control his behaviour

- He cannot be left alone

There are three rates for the care component:

- Lower – £17.10

- Middle – £43.15
- Higher – £64.50

The higher rate is paid if someone needs care or supervision during the day and night. The middle rate is paid if someone needs help during the day or night. The lower rate is paid if someone cannot cook a hot main meal or needs help for about an hour a day.

The mobility component of the Disability Living Allowance is split into two rates. The lower rate can be claimed if someone is able to walk but cannot walk outside in an unfamiliar area without guidance or supervision.

Examples of people who may be paid the lower rate

- Mr Brown is slightly confused and needs someone to help him find his way.
- Miss Pierce has agoraphobia and has panic attacks if she is outside and nobody is with her.
- Mr Heath has arthritis and dizziness. He can walk more than 100 metres, but needs to hold someone's arm.

The higher rate of the mobility component can be claimed if a person experiences the following:

- He cannot walk at all
- He is virtually unable to walk
- He is deaf and blind
- The effort of walking may be dangerous for him
- He is severely disabled and cannot control his behaviour

It is possible to claim either a care component or a mobility component or both.

Examples of people who may be paid the higher rate

- Mr Phillips has arthritis and can walk but gets pain and severe discomfort after 20 to 30 metres.
- Miss Chance has angina and severe breathing problems that are made worse by exertion.

You can help the older person claim Disability Living Allowance by requesting a DLA1A form from the Benefit Enquiry Line (tel: 0800 882 200). The helpline will send you a form and will arrange for the older person to be assessed by a doctor. The doctor will look at how fast the older person can walk, the way he walks, along with any discomfort he experiences when walking. You can also download a form from www.direct.gov.uk.

If the older person lives in a care home, he will not be able to claim Disability Living Allowance care component, because it is designed to help support people who live independently. But he will still be able to claim the mobility component if he is eligible prior to moving into the care home.

Carer's Allowance

Carer's Allowance is a benefit for people who support someone for more than 35 hours a week. It is designed to help those people who are unable to continue in full-time employment due to their caring responsibilities. However, before you try to claim this benefit, consider whether any of the following criteria may apply to your situation. In order to qualify you must:

- Be aged 16 or over
- Be caring for someone for 35 hours or more a week
- Be caring for someone who receives Attendance Allowance at either rate, or the middle or higher care component of the Disability Living Allowance, or Constant Attendance Allowance of £52.70 or more paid in conjunction with an Industrial, War or Service Pension
- Be a resident in the UK
- Have lived in the UK for 26 weeks at least during the past 12 months
- Have no immigration conditions on your stay in the UK (subject to specified exceptions)

Carer's Allowance is not means tested, which means that your savings and capital are not taken into account when you make a claim. However, it is restricted to people who are on a low income, so that you cannot claim the allowance if you earn over £87 per week, or you claim other benefits which total more than £48.65 per week (e.g. Incapacity Benefit, Retirement Pension, Severe Disability Allowance or Widow's Pension). These are known as the 'overlapping benefit rules'.

To claim Carer's Allowance, you can call the Carer's Allowance Unit on 01253 856 123, email cau.customer-services@dwp.gsi.gov.uk or download a copy of Form DS700 from www.direct.gov.uk.

The important thing to remember when claiming Carer's Allowance is that it is affected by 'overlapping benefit' rules. This means that if you claim Carer's Allowance, the person you are caring for may have his own benefits affected by that claim. If he currently receives Severe Disability Premium, he will no longer be able to claim it. It is advisable to phone an advice agency such as Counsel and Care (tel: 0845 300 7585; www.counsel andcare.org.uk) or the Carer's Allowance Unit on the number above for more information.

Carer's Premium

If you are not eligible for Carer's Allowance to be paid to you because you have an income which is more than £48.65 per week, you may be eligible to receive the Carer's Premium, which is worth £27.15 per week. You should contact the Carer's Allowance Unit on the number above to ask for more details if you are in this situation.

CHAPTER 9

Charitable help for those on a low income

THIS CHAPTER COVERS THE FOLLOWING:

- The Social Fund
- Financial help from charities
- Support with heating bills and heating maintenance
- Debt advice

Times of financial need can be stressful for anyone, regardless of their age, but being short of money in old age is becoming more and more common. There are currently over 1.5 million older people living in poverty, and the government is putting lots of energy into making sure that all of these people are helped out of poverty through welfare benefits.

Through recent media coverage, more people are hearing about how essential it is to have created savings for retirement in a personal or occupational pension scheme. However, many of today's pensioners have not received the benefit of this advice, and so have reached old age with a very low income and without the additional security of home ownership.

This chapter explains what support is available for people over 60 who are on a low income. If you are reading on behalf of an older relative, neighbour or friend, you may want to help the older person apply for a grant or a loan if he needs assistance. You should also read the previous chapter about the benefits available to older people, because it may be that the older person is not claiming everything he is entitled to. This chapter also explains what help is available if the older person is in debt.

The Social Fund

The Social Fund is money provided by the government to assist people with unplanned expenses which are difficult to meet from a low income. The Social Fund is split into two types:

1. The **Regulated Social Fund** will provide money for Cold Weather Payments, Winter Fuel Payments and funeral expenses.

2. The **Discretionary Social Fund** can provide community care grants, budgeting loans and crisis loans. Anyone can apply for this funding, but they have to show that they can meet the eligibility criteria. You can also apply on behalf of someone else, provided that the person knows that you are doing so.

The Regulated Social Fund

Money from the Regulated Social Fund covers the following funds:

- **Winter Fuel Payments:** These are payments made to any household where there is an individual over 60. A person can qualify by being 60 on the Monday of the third week in September. The payment is designed to help with the additional costs of heating and lighting during the winter months, although it does not depend on how cold the weather is. If the older person lives on his own and is 79 or under, he will receive £200. If he is under 79 and lives with his partner, the household will receive £300 between the two of them. If someone is over 80 and lives on his own, he receives £300, and if there are two people in the same household both over 80, the household receives £300. If the older person lives in a care home and is not receiving Pension Guarantee Credit, he will be eligible to receive £150 if he is over 80 and £100 if he is under 80. If he lives in a care home but receives Pension Guarantee Credit, he will not be eligible for a Winter Fuel Payment.

If the older person receives other benefits already, he will receive his Winter Fuel Payment automatically. If he does not receive any benefits but he claimed for a Winter Fuel Payment last year, he will also receive it automatically. If he has never claimed it and does not receive any benefits, he can make a claim by calling the Winter Fuel Payment Helpline (tel: 0856 915 1515).

- **Age-Related Payments:** These are payments made to people if they are over a certain age. For example, if a person is over 65 on or before the third Monday in September, he may be entitled to a one-off payment of £200 to help with living expenses, including Council Tax bills.

  The amount received depends on the person's age and whether he receives Pension Credit. If he does not receive Pension Credit and lives on his own, he will receive a payment of £200. If he has a spouse who is also over 65, he will receive a household payment of £200. If he is 65 or over and lives in a care home, he will receive £100.

  If he currently receives Pension Guarantee Credit and is over 70 in the qualifying week, he will receive £50. If he is under 70 and claims Pension Guarantee Credit, he is not eligible for any payment.

  For more details, please contact the Winter Fuel Payment Centre (tel: 029 2042 8106).

- **Cold Weather Payments:** These are made towards extra heating costs when there are periods of very cold weather. They are worth £8.50 per qualifying week and are paid when:

  - the average temperature recorded or forecast within the local area for seven consecutive days is zero degrees Celsius (freezing) or below;

  - the claimant is in receipt of Pension Credit; or

  - the claimant is receiving Disability Premium or Severe Disability Premium; or

  - he lives in his own home rather than a care home.

Payments are automatically awarded to eligible older people, but if you are concerned because you think that the older person should have received one and did not, contact the local Jobcentre Plus office. Contact details of your local office can be found in your local telephone directory, or by looking on the Jobcentre Plus website (www.jobcentreplus.gov.uk).

- **Help with funeral costs:** The Social Fund can provide money towards the cost of arranging a funeral of a partner or close relative or friend. The person claiming the funeral costs must be the person responsible for the cost of the funeral, and he should be receiving either Pension Guarantee Credit, Housing Benefit or Council Tax Benefit. The person who died must have been resident in the UK, and generally the funeral must take place in the UK.

Funds received will depend on the deceased person's estate. Enquiries on these funds should always be made before the funeral arrangements, because the amount of money given towards these costs can vary.

The funeral payment can cover:

- Necessary burial or cremation costs
- Certain necessary travel costs
- Up to £700 for other funeral expenses, such as a coffin or flowers

Claims for these funeral costs can be made by calling the Pension Service Helpline on 0845 606 0265. Often a funeral director will have a supply of the forms and may wait for payment until the grant money has been received. You will need to send the funeral director's bill in with the claim form you receive from the Pension Service, and you should normally claim within three months of the funeral. As it is a grant and not a loan, you will not have to pay the money back.

The Discretionary Social Fund

The older person can also receive money from the Discretionary Social Fund, which is split into three sections:

1. Community Care Grants
2. Budgeting loans
3. Crisis loans

These funds are administered from a central office and because available funds are often limited, there are strict rules and guidelines about who can receive the money. Applications made at the end of the financial year can often be unsuccessful because the funds have run out for the year. If you, or the older person, are thinking about making an application in February or March, it is advisable to wait until April to make the claim.

Community Care Grants

These are available to people who receive Pension Credit and they do not have to be repaid. Savings over £1,000 will be deducted from any grant made. Applications for these grants can be made at a local Pension Service or Jobcentre Plus office, and each office has a budget for making grants.

The grant must meet one of the following criteria:

- It will help a person stay in his own home rather than moving into a care home or hospital; for example, buying a fridge to store medication.

- The grant would help set up a home after a person has been in hospital, a care home, prison or hostel.

- It can help towards certain travel expenses.

- The family or claimant is under a great deal of pressure, and needs to purchase necessary items; for example, because a member of the household has a disability, he has been made homeless, there has been a close family bereavement, or a relationship has broken down and someone needs to move to a place of safety.

For instance, someone could apply for a Community Care Grant for furniture, a washing machine, cooker, bedding, carpets, clothes, removal costs or travel expenses. Travel expenses can be claimed if the older person needs to travel to a funeral, visit someone who is ill, or move to more suitable accommodation.

Assistance is not available from this fund for holidays, respite care, help at home, medical expenses, most debts or telephone installation.

There is no maximum amount that can be applied for, although someone cannot receive a grant of less than £100 unless it is for travel expenses. It is important to show that the item will help the older person remain living at home. Savings and capital over the value of £1,000 (£2,000 if the applicant is over 60) will be taken into account when a loan is being considered by staff.

To apply, the older person should complete Form SF300, which is available from your local Jobcentre Plus office or can be downloaded from www.dwp.gov.uk. When the form is completed, it is very important to stress what you will use the money for, and how the item you are applying for will help you. It may be helpful to ask a social worker, carer or doctor to write a supporting letter for the application.

The Social Fund Officer will consider the application, and will contact the applicant within 28 days. It may be that the full amount of money will be awarded, or maybe only a partial amount.

CASE STUDY

Mrs Pink is 88 and is in fairly good health. She has recently been widowed. Her cooker is broken and her home has no heating. This means that she cannot prepare hot food and her house is cold, which, in the long term, may make her ill or unable to remain in her own home. Mrs Pink is awarded a £400 Community Care Grant to buy a cooker and electric heaters.

Budgeting loans

If someone is refused a Community Care Grant, he may be awarded a budgeting loan, which is repaid weekly from benefits. To receive a budgeting loan, the older person must be receiving Pension Credit and have been receiving the benefit for the previous 26 weeks (unless he is moving out of institutional care, e.g. a care home).

Some people receiving benefits find that budgeting loans are a useful way of spreading the costs of large items, especially as there is no interest charged on the loan.

In deciding whether someone can be awarded a budgeting loan, the Social Fund Officer will look at the amount of time that he has been on benefits, the other people in his house and any previous Social Fund loans.

The maximum loan available is £1,500 and the minimum is £100. As with Community Care Grants, savings over £1,000 (or £2,000 for a couple) will reduce the amount of loan received. The most one person can owe the Social Fund at any one time is £1,500 and the older person could be refused a loan if he has one outstanding already.

Social Fund loans can be considered for similar items as the Community Care Grants; for example, furniture, household equipment, clothing and footwear, removal costs, home improvements or home maintenance.

To apply for a Social Fund loan, the older person should fill out Form SF500, available from Jobcentre Plus offices or by telephoning the Pension Service (tel: 0845 606 0265).

Crisis loans

If the older person is in urgent need of funds, he can apply for a crisis loan, available from the Social Fund. Crisis loans can be claimed by anyone regardless of whether they are in receipt of benefits. A person may be granted a crisis loan if he has emergency needs or he experiences a disaster, such as a fire or flood, and the loan is needed to prevent serious damage or risk to his health and safety. The Social Fund Officer will take into account income and savings and whether there are alternative sources of financial assistance.

To apply for a crisis loan, complete Form SF401, which can be obtained from the local Jobcentre Plus office or by telephoning the Pension Service on 0845 606 0265. It can also be downloaded from www.dwp.gov.uk. You can help the older person to apply for a loan.

Financial help from charities

Some older people cannot get help from the Social Fund because they do not receive Pension Credit or one of the other qualifying benefits. If the older person is not entitled to get help, he should consider applying for help from charities. Charities can often offer assistance to meet specific needs.

Most charities will only provide assistance if the older person is already receiving the benefits he is eligible for. Read Chapter 8 in this guide to check whether the older person is claiming all of the benefits that he is eligible for. You can help him apply if he is missing something.

Each charity has criteria governing the way they allocate grants, including:

- Whom they will assist
- What they will assist towards
- How much it will contribute
- Any limits to savings or income a person can have and still remain entitled to a grant

If the older person is trying to obtain a grant for an expensive item, such as a stairlift or structural adaptation to his home, he may find that a charity will only be able to make a small grant towards the total cost. Therefore, it may be necessary to apply to a number of charities to make up the full amount required. There are books and internet databases available, such as 'Joblink' and 'Charity Net', which provide details of charities which may provide support, depending on individual circumstances. You can also contact an advice agency such as Counsel and Care (tel: 0845 300 7585; www.counselandcare.org.uk) which has details of charities which may be able to provide assistance.

How are the charitable grants provided?

Some charities will agree to make regular weekly or monthly grants to help with ongoing expenses. You should check that the benefit being received by the older person will not be affected by the receipt of this money. The money can be used for any number of things, from buying furniture to specialist equipment. You are unlikely to be able to find charities willing to meet top-up payments for care home placements, or to pay for home care services.

Which charity should the older person apply to?

The type of charity that can provide a grant will depend on the personal circumstances of the older person. Charities will ask for information about an applicant to decide whether he is suitable, and whether they can provide assistance. They are likely to ask for the following information:

personal details, marital status, a partner's circumstances, income and savings, employment history, information about health and disabilities, religion, immigration status, where the applicant lives and whether he has any history with the armed forces.

Charities receive a large number of applications so it is important to provide as much information as possible to help them make the decision. All charities should have a confidentiality policy that they must follow so that personal information is protected.

The following categories outline what charities are most likely to support, and how they link in with someone's individual history and current circumstances:

- **Profession, trade or employment:** Some charities are linked to trades or professions and will support people with a particular employment history. For example, if the older person was a teacher, shop worker or tailor, there are charities which specifically help people who have previously been in this type of employment. The older person will need to provide his employment details; for example, the name of the employer, the address of the workplace, what work he did, the dates of his employment or the number of years that he was in that job.

- **Armed service history:** There are many charities that represent ex-members of regiments or ex-servicemen and women of a particular rank. The Soldiers, Sailors, Airmen and Families Association (SSAFA) (tel: 0845 130 0975; www.ssafa.org.uk), the Royal British Legion (tel: 0845 772 5725; www.britishlegion.org.uk) and the Royal Air Forces Association (tel: 0116 266 5224; www.rafa.org.uk) are good places to start when looking for military-related charities. SSAFA will accept applications even if the applicant only served for a short period of time or was in national service. SSAFA has local representatives who can advise anyone who has served in the forces and their dependants. It is important to provide as much detail as possible of the service, such as rank, service number and the dates that the person served.

- **Religion:** Some charities will support people of a specific religion.

- **Society, clubs or union membership:** Organisations, such as the Freemasons, or some trade unions have funds for their members and ex-members.

- **Medical:** Some charities aim to support people with a certain illness or disability. Applicants will need to explain how their illness or disability affects them and how the grant will assist them to purchase any equipment that will help them manage their day-to-day living.

- **Background:** Some charities can only help people from a specific class background. They will probably ask to see details of education, social situation or background.

- **Geographical area:** Some charities will help people who live or have lived in a specific geographical area.

There are also general funds which are available and accept applications from people. However, it is important to make applications to particular charities, such as armed service charities, trade funds, society charities, religious charities and geographical charities, before trying these other general funds because they are likely to receive a larger number of applications. General funds would be those available from charities which help people in poverty, or assist older people generally. There are a wide number of charities available and you can search for specific ones on Charity Search (www.charitychoice.co.uk).

How to locate the specific charities and funds available

It can be difficult to know what funds are available to apply to, especially if you, or the older person, have never made an application previously. The Citizens Advice Bureau, a social worker or local voluntary agency can assist you to find relevant charities that provide grants or can assist you to make applications. Counsel and Care can also help you to apply to the most suitable charities.

Making an application

Some charities are happy for individuals or their family to contact them directly. Others require a letter or phone call endorsing the application, from a social worker, doctor or other charity. This is known as a referral. Note that some doctors will make a charge for endorsing a form.

If the older person would like to make an application for assistance from a charity, you can contact the charity on his behalf to ask about the application process. The charity will be able to send you more information about how to apply. It may send you its application form or ask you to send a personal letter containing all the details that it needs to make a decision. For larger amounts or when applying to particular trusts, it may be necessary to prove certain details, with either a birth certificate, doctor's letter or evidence of income.

If the older person is asking for a grant for repairs to his home, he will have to supply quotes for the work that needs to be done. If the application is for a piece of equipment because he has a disability, he may have to supply a letter from a doctor or occupational therapist to say that the equipment is suitable and that there is no statutory funding available. Some charities, such as those who assist specific people, arrange for applicants to be visited by welfare officers in order to assess their claim. They may also be able to apply to other relevant charities on the applicants' behalf.

When to make the application

Charities vary in their timeframes for assessing applications and awarding grants. Some charity committees meet only occasionally, once a quarter for example, to decide on grants, and others may meet on a weekly basis. This should be a question that you ask before applying. If the need is immediate, it may not be appropriate to apply to charities that meet only a few times a year as the application may take some time to process.

Payment of the charitable grant

If a charity agrees to make a 'one-off' grant for an item, it may prefer to make the grant payable to the company or organisation providing the item rather than directly to the applicant. Other charities may be willing to provide the grant to the organisation applying on behalf of the older person so that it can process the grant. Most charities will require a receipt to confirm that the grant has been received and used to provide the item.

Single Needs Grants

Counsel and Care is a charity that provides advice to older people, their families and carers. It also provides charitable grants which are available on a general basis, provided that individuals meet the application criteria. Application forms can be downloaded from www.counselandcare.org.uk or by calling 0845 300 7585. Counsel and Care can also help individuals make applications to other charitable organisations, and can help make up larger amounts of money from a number of different organisations.

The grants made are up to the value of £250 per year, and to qualify someone must be over 60, and have savings of less than £2,500 (or £3,500 if they are a couple).

Support with heating bills and heating maintenance

It may be that the older person lives in a house which is badly insulated, or he has had problems with his heating system which means that he cannot keep himself warm. It may be that he is eligible for assistance with his heating or insulation improvements from the government-funded Warm Front Scheme, which can provide a package of energy-efficiency and heating arrangements to qualifying households up to a value of £2,700 in England and Wales. This is called the Warm Deal in Scotland (tel: 0800 316 6009). The Warm Front Scheme will assist households who either own or privately rent their homes and would benefit from the amendments, or where there is the greatest risk of the person suffering from lack of heating. To be eligible, someone must be over 60 and in receipt of Pension Credit or disability benefits. An organisation known as Eaga Partnership runs the scheme in most areas of England. For further information and advice, or to apply for a Warm Front Grant, call Eaga (tel: 0800 316 2808). There may also be grants, discounts or subsidised work offered through energy providers and local authorities for insulation and energy-efficiency work. The Energy Saving Trust (tel: 020 7222 0101; www.est.org.uk) will be able to help locate these.

Many fuel suppliers have charitable funds and provide grants towards fuel debt. Contact the customer services department at your fuel supplier to ask for more details about this.

Debt advice

Many older people reach retirement with debts, or they accumulate debt once they have retired because they have a low income. If you know an older person who is in this situation, you can help him seek assistance from National Debtline (tel: 0808 808 4000; www.nationaldebtline.co.uk), which can give comprehensive and confidential advice on how to cope and manage repayments, etc. You should also make sure that he is claiming all of the benefits that he is eligible for. Details of all of the benefits available to older people are available in Chapter 8 of this guide.

CHAPTER 10

If you have concerns or complaints

THIS CHAPTER COVERS THE FOLLOWING:

- First steps
- Why you may want to make a complaint
- Informal complaints
- Formal complaints
- Independent advocacy services
- Complaining about care at home
- Complaining about care in a care home
- Complaining about NHS services
- Serious complaints against a doctor or nurse

First steps

Making a complaint can feel daunting. However, in certain circumstances, it is a necessary and essential step to take. Making a complaint means that you are more likely to get services which you are happy with, and it gives the organisation you are complaining to an opportunity to improve its services. All local councils and NHS organisations must have a published complaints procedure which is made available to service users.

This chapter looks at when you can make a complaint, how to organise it, and the processes involved in the council's social services and NHS' complaints procedures. Most of the following information is relevant to England, but there will be similarities in Scotland and Wales.

Why you may want to make a complaint

If you are concerned about the quality of service the older person has been receiving or he has been refused a service, sometimes using a formal complaints procedure is the best way to challenge decisions or to improve the services he has been offered.

Your complaint could relate to any of the following:

- A decision you are unhappy with
- A concern about the quality of a service
- A delay in decision making or provision of services
- The delivery or non-delivery of services
- The quantity, frequency, change or cost of a service
- The attitude or behaviour of staff
- How the assessment and eligibility criteria have been applied
- The assessment, care management and review

Informal complaints

While most organisations have a formal complaints procedure, in many circumstances, you can resolve your complaint informally by initially raising your concerns with the relevant department or member of staff. This will give the organisation an opportunity to provide you with an explanation about what has happened or for it to reconsider its decision. However, you should not allow the organisation to delay or detract you from making a formal complaint.

If you want to raise an informal complaint, you can do this either in person or by writing a letter. You need to make sure that the organisation is provided with all the relevant information about the older person that it may need to reconsider its decision. It may not have taken all of the older person's circumstances into account when it made the decision that you are not satisfied with.

If progress is made or if your concerns are resolved, it may be that a formal complaint is not necessary. If you remain dissatisfied with the way that your concerns have been dealt with, you may want to move the complaint to the formal stage, using the organisation's complaints procedure.

CASE STUDY

Mr Green is in hospital because he has fallen over in his home and he has a suspected broken hip. He is in a lot of pain and is not sleeping very well at night. He has been placed in a bed in a ward which is very busy, and he is nearest the door. At night there is a lot of movement in the ward and the corridor outside, and he finds that this disturbs him, preventing him from going to sleep. Mr Green's wife asks a Ward Manager if it is possible for him to move beds to somewhere quieter, and she agrees.

In this example, this complaint was resolved before it really became a big issue, for either the patient, his relatives or the staff. Often a chat with someone in charge will mean that a service is changed or improved. For more serious concerns, or for ongoing unresolved issues, the complaint may need to be taken further.

Formal complaints

If you are not satisfied with the way your concerns have been dealt with, you can make a formal complaint using the official complaints procedure. Government regulations mean that local councils and the NHS must have a complaints procedure in place and they must publish details of this to users of the service.

The organisation's complaints leaflet should explain how to make a complaint and what to expect from the process. Sometimes the leaflet will have a detachable form which you can use to make your complaint. The leaflet will also explain the response timescales, so you know when to expect a reply.

Your letter should concentrate on the main facts of your concerns; for example, if you are dissatisfied with the reliability of a service, your letter should state the dates and times it was unreliable. You should keep copies of all of the letters you send or receive about your complaint for your own records.

If you make a complaint in person or by telephone, you should note down the name of the person you speak to, and ask that he sends you a letter confirming that your complaint has been received and detailing who is investigating it.

It is useful to remember that anything said in person or on the telephone may be difficult to confirm. If you feel that you have been given important facts or information by a member of staff, ask him to confirm it in writing. It is a good idea to keep a record of the telephone calls you make or receive, and to note down the name of the person you spoke with.

If a situation has arisen or an issue has been unsatisfactory for some time, involving a vulnerable person that you care for, many emotions can be generated. To resolve a complaint successfully and improve the situation, it is important to remain focused on the facts. The professionals involved have a responsibility to treat both you and the older person with respect and also to respond appropriately to your concerns; likewise, many organisations have procedures about the way service users behave towards members of staff.

Independent advocacy services

You may find in some situations that an independent advocate can help resolve issues, and help clarify communication between the older person and the professionals. If the advocate is independent, he will not be employed by the organisation that is being complained about. An independent advocate will represent the older person's views if he is unhappy about a situation or decision and can discuss with him in private and in confidence to establish what outcome he would like. With the older person's permission, the independent advocate can speak on his behalf or support him to speak for himself and to represent his views. This can be important especially for the older person if he feels unable to speak out for himself or he feels unable to challenge the people involved.

The independent advocate will not make decisions for the older person, but he will ensure that he has all the information the older person needs to be able to make an informed decision. This includes making sure that he can understand some of the complicated information that some organisations provide. He can support the older person at, or attend, meetings on his behalf.

If you want to find a local independent advocacy organisation to help the older person, you can contact the Older People's Advocacy Alliance (OPAAL) (www.opaal.org.uk).

Complaining about care at home

If you are dissatisfied about the standard of care the older person is receiving in his own home from health services, social services or a care agency, you should first speak to someone in charge of the service. This may be the manager or supervisor of the home care services, the manager of the district nurses, or the manager responsible for the social worker involved in organising the older person's care.

Which complaints process do I use?

If you are dissatisfied with the response you receive from a manager, you can make a complaint using the organisation's complaints procedure. If the service the older person receives is provided by the NHS, you will need to use the NHS complaints procedure. If the service is provided by the older person's local council's social services, you will need to use the local council's complaints procedure. If the service is arranged by you or the older person and provided by a private agency or a voluntary organisation, it should have its own internal complaints procedure. However, if the service is provided by a private or voluntary agency, but was arranged by social services following a care needs assessment, you can complain about the service using the local council's complaints procedure.

If you are complaining about home care provided by social services or a private agency, you can also complain to the Commission for Social Care Inspection (CSCI) (tel: 0845 015 0120; www.csci.org.uk). CSCI is the independent body which registers and regulates social care in England. In

Scotland this body is the Scottish Commission for the Regulation of Care, and in Wales it is the Care Standards Inspectorate for Wales. It can investigate your complaint if it concerns a National Minimum Standards issue.

Q What are National Minimum Standards?

A National Minimum Standards are a set of standards which all care agencies must meet. The standards are a legal requirement of the Care Standards Act 2000, and all care providers are inspected to see whether they are meeting these standards. Services which do not meet the standards are required to improve the aspects of their service which need changing, and can ultimately be closed if they fail to meet the standards.

If your complaint relates to abuse

If the concerns you have relate to a form of abuse (e.g. theft, negligence, physical or emotional abuse), it should be reported to the local council's social services Protection of Vulnerable Adults (POVA) co-ordinator. The POVA co-ordinator has a responsibility to investigate any alleged abuse and to check that the staff members had been fully checked on employment. Before members of staff start work with vulnerable adults they have to be checked against the POVA register and the Criminal Records Bureau (CRB) and anyone with a history of abuse would not be employed. If a member of staff commits abuse in this environment, he would be reported to POVA and the CRB, and would be prevented from working in a similar environment in the future. You can still use the normal complaints process to report abuse, and the council will refer it to the right people.

Complaining about care in a care home

All care homes are required to have a complaints procedure in place in accordance with the Care Standards Act 2000. They must also ensure that all residents have access to this procedure.

You, or the resident himself, can begin by making your concerns known to the care home manager or matron. You could also ask another member of staff to speak to him on your behalf.

If you are not satisfied with the response you receive or any attempts to resolve your concerns, or you do not want to discuss the complaint with the staff at the home, you can make a complaint to an inspection officer at the CSCI. CSCI can investigate your complaint if it relates to a National Minimum Standards issue. You can write or speak to the inspectors in confidence, but confidentiality may be difficult to maintain if they are to investigate particular events or circumstances to a full resolution. You do not have to tell the home that you have made a complaint to CSCI, but you may wish to do so, so that the home is aware that you are taking your concerns seriously and that you are aware of your right to do so.

If your complaint does not relate to a National Minimum Standards issue, you should use the complaints procedure of the home the older person is in. If the older person is financially supported in the home by his local council's social services, you can use its complaints procedure to take your issues forward if you feel that they have not been resolved. If the older person funds his own placement in the care home and you feel that the home's complaints procedure has not resolved your concerns, you may wish to check the older person's contract with the care home to check whether the terms he has agreed to are being breached. If this is the case, you may wish to contact the Office of Fair Trading for advice. If your complaint does not relate to the National Minimum Standards not being met or the contract terms being breached, you may wish to think about moving the older person into a different care home. You may also wish to consider involving an independent advocate to help you resolve your complaint.

Complaining about NHS services

All health services are required to have published complaints procedures to enable their patients to raise concerns. The older person's local Primary Care Trust (PCT) will be able to give you a copy of this, or you can pick it up at his local GP surgery or walk-in clinic.

Complaints about services or treatment provided by the NHS using the NHS complaints procedure must be made within certain time limits:

- Within six months of the event you wish to complain about; or

- Within six months of finding out about the right to complain, providing it is within 12 months of the event.

A complaint made outside these time limits may be accepted if you can demonstrate that there is a good reason for not complaining before this date.

Complaints can be made to any member of NHS staff by you as long as the older person has given his permission for you to complain on his behalf. If the older person wants to complain himself, he may request support to make a complaint from an independent advocate.

The NHS complaints procedure has the following stages:

Informal resolution

You should first try to resolve your complaint with the staff member or team who is providing the older person's healthcare. The older person's local Patient Advice and Liaison Service (PALS) should help you try to resolve the complaint quickly so that you do not have to take the complaint further. The PALS should also act as one of the gateways to local independent advice and advocacy for you if you feel that you need the support to make a formal complaint.

> **Q What do PALSs do?**
>
> **A** All Primary Care Trusts and health organisations have PALSs to support patients, and their relatives and carers. They can provide information and advice about the services available in the older person's local area, and they can help you access independent support if a complaint is necessary. PALSs should use the feedback that they get from patients and their carers to improve the services in that local area.

Local resolution

This is the first stage of the formal complaints procedure. You can make a formal complaint to the named Complaints Manager at the PCT. The Complaints Manager is responsible for dealing with written complaints on behalf of the Chief Executive of the Trust.

You should receive a response to your complaint from the PCT within 25 working days of your making the complaint. This may need to be extended if the older person's case is particularly complex, but the PCT should ask your permission. If your complaint remains unresolved for more than six months, you can refer it directly to the Healthcare Commission – the regulatory body for health organisations.

NHS Foundation Trusts may have a different procedure at local resolution stage, and you should contact them to ask how to raise a complaint if the older person's care has been provided by them. The Independent Review stage (see below) does apply to NHS Foundation Trusts.

Independent Review

If you are not happy with the outcome of the local resolution, you can request to arrange for your complaint to be heard by an Independent Review panel. This is organised by contacting the Healthcare Commission – the regulatory body for all healthcare providers. You must make your request to the Healthcare Commission no later than six months after you have received the outcome of the local resolution stage of the complaints process.

You can contact the Healthcare Commission at Freepost NAT 18958, Complaints Investigation Team, Manchester M1 9XZ, on the website www.healthcarecommission.org.uk or by calling 0845 601 3012.

If an Independent Review panel is arranged to hear your complaint, you should receive details about the results of its investigations, conclusions and suggestions. You should also have the opportunity to check a draft report and make comments. There is a target time of six months for the whole review panel process to be completed.

The Health Service Ombudsman

If you disagree with the findings of the review panel, you can refer your complaint to the Health Service Ombudsman (HSO). The HSO is completely independent of the NHS and the government.

The Ombudsman is able to investigate complaints about:

- 'Maladministration' – that is, poor administration or the wrong application of the rules.

- 'Clinical judgement' – an inappropriate action or decision made by a member of staff. Complaints concerning clinical judgement can only be made for incidents occurring after April 1996.

The Ombudsman will not investigate your complaint until you have exhausted the formal NHS complaints procedure first.

A complaint made about NHS care should usually be made within 12 months of the event occurring, unless there are special reasons (e.g. if you are late making a complaint because of delays in the NHS' complaints procedure).

You can contact the Health Service Ombudsman at Millbank Tower, Millbank, London SW1P 4QP, on its website www.ombudsman.org.uk or by calling 0845 015 4033.

Serious complaints against a doctor or nurse

If you have a complaint that may be serious enough to justify removing a nurse's or health staff's professional registration, you can make a complaint to the Nursing and Midwifery Council (tel: 020 7637 7181; www.nmc-uk.org). This is the regulatory body for nursing, midwifery and health visiting and is set up to establish and improve standards of nursing in order to serve and protect the public. It investigates complaints against nurses, midwives and health visitors and it has the power to remove their professional registration, if necessary.

If you have a complaint about the older person's GP, you should first contact his GP surgery, as all GP practices must have a complaints procedure. You can also contact the PALS at his local hospital, or write to the Complaints Manager at his local Primary Care Trust (all contact details for local organisations will be available in the telephone directory, or at local libraries).

If you have a serious complaint about a doctor, you can also complain to his professional organisation – the General Medical Council (GMC). The GMC has the legal power to investigate doctors working in the UK and can take a range of actions. To make a complaint to the GMC, you can write or call its complaints department (tel: 0845 357 3456; www.gmc-uk.org).

Appendix

Useful addresses

This Appendix contains details about agencies and organisations which you may find useful. They will be able to provide further information about the issues you are interested in. If you are unsure who to contact, please call the Counsel and Care advice line on 0845 300 7585. Please be aware that inclusion of organisations does not constitute a recommendation.

Abbeyfield Society

A volunteer-led charity providing housing with care to older people.

Abbeyfield House
53 Victoria Street
St Albans
Hertfordshire AL1 3UW

Tel: 01727 857 536
Email: post@abbeyfield.com
Website: www.abbeyfield.com

Action for Advocacy

A resource for advocacy groups which facilitates the growth of new schemes. It may be able to signpost you to particular advocacy groups in a local area.

PO Box 31856
Lorrimore Square
London SE17 3XR

Tel: 020 7820 7868
Email: info@actionforadvocacy.org.uk
Website: www.actionforadvocacy.org.uk

Action on Elder Abuse

Raises awareness of all aspects of elder abuse, including abuse in residential care. This organisation also runs a dedicated phone line.

Astral House
1268 London Road
London SW16 4ER

Tel: 0808 808 8141
Email: enquiries@elderabuse.org.uk
Website: www.elderabuse.org.uk

Advice Information and Mediation Service for Retirement Housing (AIMS)

Gives advice and mediation on a range of problems encountered by people living in sheltered and other forms of retirement housing.

Age Concern England
Astral House
1268 London Road
London SW16 4ER

Tel: 020 8765 7465
Advice line: 0845 600 2001
Email: aims@ace.org.uk
Website: www.ageconcern.org.uk/aims

Advisory Conciliation and Arbitration Service (ACAS)

Offers employment resolution services to employers and employees.

Brandon House
180 Borough High Street
London SE1 1LW

Tel: 0845 747 4747
Website: www.acas.org.uk

Advocacy Resource Exchange

An organisation which can locate advocacy resources in your local area.

PO Box 282
Broxbourne EN11 1AS

Tel: 0845 122 8633
Email: helpline@advocacyresource.net
Website: www.advocacyresource.net

Age Concern Cymru

Holds details of the health and social care system in Wales. It can advise on benefits and other information. Local Age Concern groups can provide details of organisations which provide face-to-face support and services.

Ty John Pathy
13/14 Neptune Court

Tel: 029 2043 1555
Email: enquiries@accymru.org.uk

Vanguard Way
Cardiff CF24 5PJ

Website: www.accymru.org.uk

Age Concern England

Holds details of the health and social care system in England. It can advise on benefits and other information. Local Age Concern groups can provide details of organisations which provide face-to-face support and services. It provides a number of useful fact sheets.

Astral House
1268 London Road
London SW16 4ER

Tel: 0800 009 966
Website: www.ageconcern.org.uk

Age Concern Scotland

Holds details of the health and social care system in Scotland. It can advise on benefits and other information. Local Age Concern groups can provide details of organisations which provide face-to-face support and services.

Causewayside House
160 Causewayside
Edinburgh EH9 1PR

Scottish Helpline for Older
People: 0845 125 9732
Email: enquiries@acscot.org.uk
Website: www.ageconcernscotland.
org.uk

Al Anon

Al Anon family groups provide support to anyone who has been affected by someone else's drinking.

61 Great Dover Street
London SE1 4YF

Tel: 020 7403 0888
Email: enquiries@al-anonuk.org.uk
Website: www.al-anonuk.org.uk

Alcoholics Anonymous

An organisation which helps people who have alcohol dependency and who are seeking help. It can support people of all ages.

General Service Office
PO Box 1
10 Toft Green
York YO1 7ND

Helpline: 0845 769 7555
Email: aanewcomer@runbox.com
Website: www.alcoholics-anonymous.
org.uk

Alzheimer's Scotland

The corresponding organisation of the Alzheimer's Society for Scotland.

22 Drumsheugh Gardens
Edinburgh EH3 7RN

Tel: 0808 808 3000
Email: alzheimer@alzscot.org
Website: www.alzscot.org

Alzheimer's Society

Publishes leaflets and gives information and advice to people who live with dementia and their carers. It can provide details of local groups and campaigns on behalf of people with dementia.

Gordon House
10 Greencoat Place
London SW1P 1PH

Tel: 0845 300 0336
Email: info@alzhemiers.org.uk
Website: www.alzheimers.org.uk

Anchor Staying Put

Provides guidance and assistance to carry out repairs, improvements or adaptations necessary to help people continue living in their own homes.

Burnbank House
Balliol Business Park
Benton Lane
Longbenton
Newcastle-upon-Tyne NE12 8EW

Tel: 0191 270 6069
Email: ann.young@anchor.org.uk
Website: www.stayingput.org.uk

Arthritis Care

An organisation providing information about arthritis through the helpline. It can also put people in touch with local groups which support both those with arthritis and their carers.

18 Stephenson Way
London NW1 2HD

Helpline: 0808 800 4050
Email: info@arthritiscare.org.uk
Website: www.arthritiscare.org.uk

Association of Charity Officers

An umbrella organisation offering information about charitable help and which can put you in touch with the most relevant charity for your needs.

Five Ways

Tel: 01707 651 777

57–59 Hatfield Road
Potters Bar
Hertfordshire EN6 1HS

Email: info@aco.uk.net
Website: www.aco.uk.net

Attendance Allowance Helpline

Provides information about this non-means-tested benefit for over-65s and it can help you make a claim.

Tel: 0845 712 3456

Benefit Enquiry Line

Provides advice and information for people on a low income and with disabilities, along with their carers and representatives, about social security benefits and how to claim them.

Tel: 0800 882 200

Benefit Enquiry Line (Northern Ireland)

Can help with enquiries about benefits, benefits calculation, and the completion of forms.

Tel: 0800 220 674

Bridgefast

An independent property and sales management company that will organise the sale of property belonging to people moving into a care home. It supports people who have no carers or relatives to help them, but it can also help carers do this.

Bridgefast Management Ltd
Copenhagen Court
32 New Street
Basingstoke
Hampshire RG21 7DT

Tel: 0845 053 0089
Email: enquiries@bridgefast.co.uk
Website: www.bridgefast.co.uk

British Association for Counselling and Psychotherapy (BACP)

A membership organisation for counsellors. The BACP will provide a list of counsellors in your area.

BACP House

Tel: 0870 443 5252

15 St John's Business Park
Lutterworth
Leicestershire LE17 4HB

Email: bacp@bacp.co.uk
Website: www.bacp.co.uk

British Heart Foundation

Gives advice and information about heart conditions, as well as funding research, education and care.

14 Fitzhardinge Street
London W1H 6DH

Tel: 0845 070 8070
Email: internet@bhf.org.uk
Website: www.bhf.org.uk

British Red Cross

Offers a range of services, including care in the home and transport assistance. It can provide details of loan services for equipment, such as wheelchairs.

UK Office
44 Moorfields
London EC2Y 9AL

Tel: 0870 170 7000
Email: information@redcross.org.uk
Website: www.redcross.org.uk

Care & Repair Cymru

Provides information about home improvements in Wales and how to arrange these if you have no local Home Improvement Agency in your area.

Norbury House
Norbury Road
Fairwater
Cardiff CF5 3AS

Tel: 029 2057 6286
Email: enquiries@careandrepair.org.uk
Website: www.careandrepair.org.uk

Care & Repair England

Provides information about home improvements in England and how to arrange these if you have no local Home Improvement Agency in your area.

The Renewal Trust Business
Centre
3 Hawksworth Street
Nottingham NG3 2EG

Email: catrionasaxton@careandrepair-england.org.uk
Website: www.careandrepair-england.org.uk

Care & Repair Scotland

Provides information about home improvements in Scotland and how to arrange these if you have no local Home Improvement Agency in your area.

135 Buchanan Street
Suite 2.5
Glasgow G1 2JA

Tel: 0141 221 9879
Email: forum@care-repair-scot.org.uk
Website: www.careandrepairscotland.co.uk

Care Standards Inspectorate for Wales

Responsible for regulating and monitoring care services provided by care homes and home care agencies in Wales. It can also arrange for the investigation of complaints about these services.

National Assembly for Wales
Cardiff Bay
Cardiff CF99 1NA

Tel: 0845 010 5500
Email: csiw.no@wales.gsi.gov.uk
Website: www.csiw.wales.gov.uk/index.asp

Careline UK

A confidential crisis telephone line for children, young people and adults. The line is open Monday to Friday, 10am–1pm and 7pm–10pm.

Tel: 0845 122 8622

Carer's Allowance Unit

Contact the Unit for more details about Carer's Allowance and making an application for this benefit.

Palatine House
Lancaster Road
Preston
Lancashire PR1 1NS

Tel: 01253 856 123
Advice line: 0845 122 8622
Website: www.dwp.gov.uk

Carers UK

Provides advice, information and support to carers and can provide details of your local carers group.

20–25 Glasshouse Yard
London EC1A 4JT

Tel: 020 7490 8818
CarersLine: 0808 808 7777
Email: info@carersuk.org
Website: www.carersuk.org/Home

Cinnamon Trust

Provides information about keeping a pet in old age. It has details of care homes which will allow people to take pets and it can arrange for pets to be cared for if someone dies or can no longer look after them.

10 Market Square
Hayle
Cornwall TR27 4HE

Tel: 01736 757 900
Email: admin@cinnamon.org.uk
Website: www.cinnamon.org.uk

Citizens Advice Bureau (CAB)

This contact will be able to provide the number of your local CAB service. CAB provides independent advice on a wide range of issues, including benefits and debt law.

115–123 Pentonville Road
London N1 9LZ

Tel: 020 7833 2181
Website: www.adviceguide.org.uk

Commission for Social Care Inspection (CSCI)

Responsible for regulating and monitoring care services provided by care homes and home care agencies in England. It can also arrange for the investigation of complaints about these services.

33 Greycoat Street
London SW1P 2QF

Tel: 0845 015 0120
Email: enquiries@csci.gsi.gov.uk
Website: www.csci.org.uk

Community Legal Service (CLS)

Helps people find the right legal information and advice to solve problems. Counsel and Care is affiliated to the CLS.

Tel: 0845 345 4 345 (*for general advice*)
Tel: 0845 608 1122 (*to find a solicitor*)
Website: www.clsdirect.org.uk

Community Service Volunteers (CSV)

Can give information about volunteering. It provides training and it will find volunteers.

237 Pentonville Road
London N1 9NJ

Tel: 020 7278 6601
Email: information@csv.org.uk
Website: www.csv.org.uk

Consumer Credit Counselling Service

A charity providing free debt advice for people of all ages. Helpline advisers can offer immediate help, self-help material and access to counselling appointments. The service will help negotiate with lenders, if necessary.

Wade House
Merrion Centre
Leeds LS2 8NG

Helpline: 0800 138 11 11
Email: contactus@cccs.co.uk
Website: www.cccs.co.uk

Consumer Direct

An organisation giving information and advice to consumers to help them choose the right products and services. It also deals with complaints about traders. It is funded by the Department of Trade and Industry.

Tel: 0845 404 0506

Website: www.consumerdirect.gov.uk

Contact the Elderly

A national voluntary organisation which provides companionship and outings for older people who live alone.

15 Henrietta Street
Covent Garden
London WC2E 8QG

Tel: 0800 716 543
Website: www.contact-the-elderly.org

Continence Foundation

A confidential advice and fact sheet service to help people who have any bladder or bowel problems. It can put you in touch with a professional adviser.

307 Hatton Square
16 Baldwins Gardens
London EC1N 7RJ

Tel: 0845 345 0165
Email: continence-help@dial.pipex.com
Website: www.continence-foundation.org.uk

Counsel and Care

Offers advice and support for people over 60, their relatives and carers. It covers all issues, including the community care system, healthcare, hospital treatment and discharge, benefits, advocacy, living independently at home, and applying for grants and other charitable funding.

Twyman House

Helpline: 0845 300 7585

16 Bonny Street   Email: advice@counselandcare.org.uk
London NW1 9PG   Website: www.counselandcare.org.uk

Court of Protection

Arranges for the finances of people who lack mental capacity to be secured and spent on their behalf.

Public Guardianship Office   Tel: 0845 330 2900
Archway Tower   Email: custserv@guardianship.gsi.gov.uk
2 Junction Road   Website: www.guardianship.gov.uk
London N19 5SZ

Cruse Bereavement Care

Offers advice and information on bereavement. It also publishes leaflets and has counsellors to answer letters and calls.

Cruse House   Tel: 0870 167 1677
126 Sheen Road   Email: helpline@cruse.org.uk
Richmond   Website: www.crusebereavement
Surrey TW9 1UR   care.org.uk

Department for Work and Pensions

The government department which runs the pension system in the UK. You can contact it for benefit claim forms. If your enquiry is pension related, call the Pension Services at 0845 606 0265. If your enquiry relates to other benefits, call the Benefit Enquiry Line on 0800 882 200.

Public Enquiry Office   Website: www.dwp.gov.uk
Room 112
The Adelphi
1–11 John Adam Street
London WC2N 6HT

Department for Work and Pensions – Pensions Overseas Directorate

Helps with enquiries about moving abroad or back to the UK, and the arrangements for benefits. It can also deal with issues affecting the payment of benefits to those who live overseas.

Overseas Department   Tel: 0191 218 2828

Tyneview Park   Tel: 00 44 191 218 7777 (*from abroad*)
Whitley Road   Website: www.dwp.gov.uk
Benton
Newcastle-upon-Tyne NE98 1BA

Disability Law Service

Provides free telephone advice for disabled people, their families and carers. It provides specialist support for advocates and advisers of disabled people.

39–45 Cavell Street   Tel: 020 7791 9800
London E1 2BP   Email: advice@dls.org.uk
                                Website: www.dls.org.uk

Disabled Living Centres Council

Has information about Disabled Living Centres throughout the UK, and is the national voice for independent living. Disabled Living Centres give information and advice about products which can enable disabled and older people to live independently.

Redbank House   Tel: 0870 760 1580
4 St Chad's Street   Email: dlcc@dlcc.co.uk
Manchester M8 8QQ   Website: www.dlcc.co.uk

Disabled Living Foundation

Assists older and disabled people to find suitable equipment to help them achieve greater mobility and independence. Bathroom aids and adaptations can be bought directly from its website.

380–384 Harrow Road   Helpline: 0845 130 9177
London W9 2HU   Email: info@dlf.org.uk
                               Website: www.dlf.org.uk

Eaga

Information relating to getting grants for insulation and heating improvements, including the instalment of central heating. It administers the Warm Front Grants.

Eaga House   Tel: 0800 316 2808
Archbold Terrace   Website: www.eagagroup.com
Newcastle-upon-Tyne NE2 1DB

Elderly Accommodation Counsel

Information and advice about all forms of accommodation including care homes and housing with care for older people to rent or buy in all parts of the UK.

3rd Floor
89 Albert Embankment
London SE1 7TP

Tel: 020 7820 1343
Email: enquiries@e-a-c.demon.co.uk
Website: www.housingcare.org

Energy Saving Trust

Provides information about energy grants and discounts available for older people, as well as energy-efficient measures you can take.

21 Dartmouth Street
London SW1H 9BP

Tel: 020 7222 0101
Website: www.est.org.uk

Far East Prisoners of War Association

An association giving help and advice to Far Eastern prisoners of war, as well as providing a welfare service.

National Welfare Adviser
Steve Cairns OBE
136 Taunton Road
North Petherton
Bridgewater
Somerset TA6 6NN

Tel: 01278 663 127
Email: fepow@btinternet.com
Website: www.fepow.org.uk

Financial Services Authority

An independent non-governmental body which regulates the financial sector including companies providing financial plans for pensions and payment of care home fees.

25 The North Colonnade
Canary Wharf
London E14 5HS

Consumer helpline: 0845 606 1234
Website: www.fsa.gov.uk

Fold Staying Put

The co-ordinating body for Home Improvement Agencies in Northern Ireland.

Fold Housing Trust
3–6 Redburn Square
Holywood BT18 9HZ

Tel: 0289 042 8314
Email: info@foldgroup.co.uk
Website: www.foldgroup.co.uk

For Dementia (previously Dementia Relief Trust)

Gives support to carers of people with dementia. It also runs the Admiral Nurse Service. This is a service specialising in caring for a person with dementia and is available in certain areas. The helpline is open on Tuesdays, 10am–4pm and 6pm–9pm, and on Thursdays, 6pm–9pm.

6 Camden High Street
London NW1 0JH

Helpline: 0845 257 9406
Email: direct@fordementia.org.uk
Website: www.fordementia.org.uk

Foundations

The national co-ordinating body for Housing Improvement Agencies, which can locate an agency in your local area.

Bleaklow House
Howard Town Mill
Glossop
Derbyshire SK13 8HT

Tel: 01457 891 909
Email: foundations@cel.co.uk
Website: www.foundations.uk.com

Friends of the Elderly

Has day centres and care homes. It also provides home care and charitable help in certain parts of the UK.

40–42 Ebury Street
London SW1W 0LZ

Tel: 020 7730 8263
Email: enquiries@fote.org.uk
Website: www.fote.org.uk

General Medical Council (GMC)

GMC will investigate when it is alleged that doctors are not fit to practise. It will not deal with other complaints but these can be directed to the Health Service Ombudsman.

Fitness to Practise Directorate
178 Great Portland Street
London W1N 6JE

General enquiries: 0845 357 3456
Email: gmc@gmc-uk.org
Website: www.gmc-uk.org

Health Service Ombudsman

Will investigate complaints about NHS care that cannot be resolved at a local level.

The Parliamentary and
Health Service Ombudsman
Millbank Tower
Millbank
London SW1P 4QP

Tel: 0845 015 4033
Email: phso.enquiries@ombudsman.
org.uk
Website: www.ombudsman.org.uk

Help the Aged

Offers advice and help on many issues relating to older people, including benefits and accommodation. It also campaigns against age discrimination and for better universal services. It provides a number of useful fact sheets.

207–211 Pentonville Road
London N1 9UZ

'Seniorline': 0808 800 6565
Email: info@helptheaged.org.uk
Website: www.helptheaged.org.uk

Heyday

A membership organisation for retired people, offering inspiration, information and opportunities for them to take up.

Tel: 0845 888 2222 (*for membership*)
Tel: 0845 888 4444 (*for help and customer services*)
Email: customerservices@heyday.org.uk
Website: www.heyday.org.uk

Holiday Care

Provides information about transport, accommodation, visitor attractions, activity holidays and respite care establishments, particularly relating to the needs of older people.

The Hawkins Suite
Enham Place
Enham Alamein
Andover SP11 6JS

Tel: 0845 124 9974
Email: info@tourismforall.org.uk
Website: www.holidaycare.org.uk

Home Heat Helpline

Offers impartial advice to low income households about what can be done to help people keep their home warm and well insulated during the winter. The helpline is also dedicated to helping people who experience fuel poverty.

Tel: 0800 33 66 99   Website: www.homeheathelpline.org

Home Improvement Trust

This trust may be able to help if you want to release equity, specifically to pay for repairs, improvements or adaptations.

7 Mansfield Road   Tel: 0115 934 9511
Nottingham NG1 3FB   Email: info@hitrust.org
                          Website: www.improvementtrust.
                          fsbusiness.co.uk

Homeshare

A co-ordinating scheme that can match a 'homesharer' with a tenant who provides an agreed amount of support in exchange for housing.

54 Christchurch Street   Tel: 020 7351 3851
London SW3 4AR   Email: HI@homeshare.org
                           Website: www.homeshare.org

Housing Corporation

A regulator of social housing in the UK. It can provide lists of sheltered housing schemes.

1 Park Lane   Tel: 0845 230 7000
Leeds LS3 1EP   Email: enquiries@housingcorp.gsx.gov.uk
                          Website: www.housingcorp.gov.uk

Housing Mobility and Exchange Service

An organisation which works with registered social landlords and local authorities offering a range of services to help tenants move house. This includes people who have special needs or disabilities.

242 Vauxhall Bridge Road   Tel: 0845 606 6161
London SW1V 1AU   Email: customer.services@homes.org.uk
                          Website: www.direct.gov.uk/socialhousing

IFA Care

A voluntary organisation of Independent Financial Advisers who specialise in giving advice about the funding of long-term care fees.

Suite 5, Shrubbery House	Tel: 01562 822 955
21 Birmingham Road	Email: info@ifacare.co.uk
Kidderminster	Website: www.ifacare.co.uk
Worcestershire DY10 2BX	

IFA Promotions

Holds details of Independent Financial Advisers across the country.

2nd Floor	Tel: 0800 085 3250
117 Farringdon Road	Email: contact@ifap.org.uk
London EC1R 3BX	Website: www.unbiased.co.uk

Incontact

Produces quarterly newsletters and gives information and support on continence issues.

United House	Tel: 0870 770 3246
North Road	Email: info@incontact.org
London N7 9DP	Website: www.incontact.org

Independent Age

Can assist older people on low incomes by providing regular and emergency grants, aids and adaptations, and help with care home fees.

6 Avonmore Road	Tel: 020 7605 4200
London W14 8RL	Email: david.daby@independentage.org.uk
	Website: www.independentage.org.uk

Independent Complaints Advocacy Service (ICAS)

The public body involved in ensuring members of the public are involved in decision making about health and health services. It can provide access to an independent complaints advocacy service.

The Commission for Patient	Tel: 0845 120 7111
and Public Involvement in	Email: enquiries@cppih.org
Health	Website: www.cppih.org/icas.html

The Help Desk
7th Floor, 120 Edmund Street
Birmingham B3 2ES

Independent Living

Provides information about aids and adaptations for use in the home.

11 Hale Lane   Website: www.independentliving.co.uk
Mill Hill
London NW7 3NU

International Pension Centre

A team within the Department for Work and Pensions which can deal with overseas enquiries about UK benefits for overseas customers.

Tel: 0191 218 7777

Intune

A financial advice service offering a range of products for older people. It can provide quotations and information about home, car and travel insurance and personal finances. All profits go to Help the Aged.

207–221 Pentonville Road   Tel: 020 7239 1991
London N1 9UZ   Website: www.intunegroup.co.uk

Jobcentre Plus

Holds Social Fund loan forms and grant forms. There are local offices and telephone numbers around the country. Look in your local telephone directory to find your nearest office.

Correspondence Manager   Website: www.jobcentreplus.gov.uk
Jobcentre Plus Secretariat
Ground Floor, Steel City House
West Street
Sheffield S1 2GQ

Joint Council for the Welfare of Immigrants

Advice, information and representation on immigration, refugee issues and nationality. The helpline is open on Tuesdays and Thursdays, 2–5pm.

115 Old Street
London EC1V 9RT

Tel: 020 7251 8708
Email: info@jcwi.org.uk
Website: www.jcwi.org.uk

Local Government Ombudsman (LGO)

Investigates complaints about council social services. The complaints must generally have been through the social services' complaints procedures before the LGO will take on a case.

10th Floor
Millbank Tower
Millbank
London SW1P 4QP

Tel: 020 7217 4620
Website: www.lgo.org.uk

Macmillan Cancer Relief

A national charity which works to improve the quality of life of people living with cancer. It can provide palliative care nursing.

89 Albert Embankment
London SE1 7UQ

Tel: 0808 808 2020
Email: cancerline@macmillan.org.uk
Website: www.macmillan.org.uk

Mind (National Association for Mental Health)

Gives advice on any issues surrounding mental health and mental illness to individuals and their carers. It provides a number of useful fact sheets.

15–19 Broadway
London E15 4BQ

Infoline: 0845 766 0163
Email: contact@mind.org.uk
Website: www.mind.org.uk

Mobility Advice and Information Service (MAVIS)

Part of the Department for Transport which can give information and advice about wheelchair accessible vehicles, car adaptations and conversions, driving assessments, etc. It publishes a range of fact sheets about these issues.

Crowthorne Business Estate
Old Wokingham Road
Crowthorne
Berkshire RG45 6XD

Tel: 01344 661 000
Email: mavis@dft.gsi.gov.uk
Website: www.dft.gov.uk/transport
foryou/access/mavis

Motability

Holds details of mobility schemes for the disabled. These schemes can arrange adapted cars or electric wheelchairs for people receiving mobility allowance.

Wheelchair and Scooter
Scheme
Route 2 Mobility
Newbury Road
Enham Alamein
Andover
Hampshire SP11 6JS

Tel: 0845 607 6260
Website: www.motability.co.uk

National Care Association

Provides information for care professionals and members of the public about the independent care sector.

45–49 Leather Lane
London EC1N 1TJ

Tel: 020 7831 7090
Email: info@ncha.gb.com
Website: www.nca.gb.com

National Centre for Independent Living

An organisation run by and for disabled people promoting independent living and the use of direct payments. It provides information on personal assistance schemes across the UK.

4th Floor
Hampton House
20 Albert Embankment
London SE1 7TJ

Tel: 020 7587 1663
Email: info@ncil.org.uk
Website: www.ncil.org.uk

National Federation of Shopmobility

Gives advice about aids and mobility scooters available to people with a disability. The website can be searched to find local outlets.

PO Box 6641
Christchurch BH23 9DQ

Tel: 0845 644 2446
Email: info@shopmobility.org
Website: www.justmobility.co.uk/shop

NHS 24

Provides a telephone health advice and information service for people in Scotland.

Tel: 08454 24 24 24   Website: www.nhs24.com

NHS Direct

Provides information about NHS treatments and services. Health advice and diagnosis can be obtained via the telephone helpline. It can also give you details of your local Primary Care Trust or Strategic Health Authority.

7th Floor   Tel: 0845 46 47
207 Old Street   Website: www.nhsdirect.nhs.uk
London EC1V 9NR

Nursing Home Fees Agency (NHFA)

Independent Financial Advisers who can provide information about care home fees and funding a place in a care home. It can also advise on long-term insurance policies for care home fees.

NHFA Freepost (SCE12765)   Advice line: 0800 998 833
St Leonards House   Email: enquiries@nhfa.co.uk
Mill Street   Website: www.nhfa.co.uk
Eynsham
Oxford OX29 4JX

Nursing and Midwifery Council

The regulatory body for the nursing and midwifery profession.

23 Portland Place   Tel: 020 7637 7181
London W1B 1PZ   Website: www.nmc-uk.org

Office of Fair Trading

Gives advice about trading laws and buyers' rights including care home contract terms and conditions.

Enquiries Unit   Tel: 0845 722 4499
Fleetbank House   Email: enquiries@oft.gsi.gov.uk
2–6 Salisbury Square   Website: www.oft.gov.uk
London EC4Y 8JX

Older People's Advocacy Alliance (OPAAL)

OPAAL can provide details of local advocacy organisations, and provide strategic direction for the growth of new advocacy groups.

Beth Johnson Foundation
Parkfield House
64 Princes Road
Hartshill
Stoke on Trent ST4 7JL

Tel: 01782 844 036
Email: jo@bjf.org.uk
Website: www.opaal.org.uk

Parkinson's Disease Society

Advice and information for people with Parkinson's disease and their carers. It also has information about local support groups.

215 Vauxhall Bridge Road
London SW1V 1EJ

Tel: 0808 800 0303
Email: enquiries@parkinsons.org.uk
Website: www.parkinsons.org.uk

Patients Association

Provides patients with an opportunity to raise concerns and share experiences of healthcare. It can provide advice and support about making a complaint about healthcare services.

PO Box 935
Harrow
Middlesex HA1 3YJ

Tel: 0845 608 4455
Website: www.patients-association.com

Penderel's Trust

Staff can support service users who have been given a direct payment by social services for their care. This support includes advice about employer's liability insurance, recruitment, management of care money and information about paying staff. The head office number can put individuals in contact with support.

Seven Stars Estate
Wheler Road
Whitley
Coventry CV3 4LB

Tel: 0845 0500 862
Email: enquiries@penderelstrust.org.uk
Website: www.eiro.co.uk/ptnew/
index.htm

Pension Credit Application Line

To apply for Pension Credit, or to deal with enquiries about Pension Credit.

Tel: 0800 99 1234

Pension Tracing Service

Helps locate pension funds which people may have lost contact with. It can be used to find occupational and personal pension schemes. Call the number below for more details, and ask to be sent a form to complete in order to carry out a search for funds.

The Pension Service   Tel: 0845 600 2537
Tyneview Park
Whitley Road
Newcastle-upon-Tyne NE98 1BA

Pet Fostering Service Scotland

Provides temporary assistance for pet owners and their pets if the owners need to go into hospital or can no longer look after their animals.

Tel: 01877 331 496   Website: www.pfss.org.uk

The Princess Royal Trust for Carers

The largest provider of comprehensive carers support services in the UK.

142 Minories   Tel: 020 7480 7788 (*English office*)
London EC3N 1LB   Tel: 0141 221 5066 (*Scottish office*)
     Tel: 01792 472 908 (*Welsh office*)
     Email: info@carers.org
     Website: www.carers.org

Public Concern at Work

Gives free confidential legal advice to people with concerns about malpractice at work. You can remain anonymous.

Suite 301   Tel: 020 7404 6609
16 Baldwin Gardens   Email: helpline@pcaw.co.uk
London EC1N 7RJ   Website: www.pcaw.co.uk

Public Guardianship Office

The administrative arm of the Court of Protection which registers Powers of Attorney.

Archway Tower
2 Junction Road
London N19 5SZ

Tel: 0845 330 2900
Email: custserv@guardianship.gsi.gov.uk
Website: www.guardianship.gov.uk

Public Services Ombudsman for Wales

The Ombudsman considers complaints about public bodies in Wales, including local government, the NHS and GPs, and the National Assembly for Wales.

1 Ffordd yr Hen Gae
Pencoed CF35 5LJ

Tel: 01656 641 150
Email: ask@ombudsman-wales.org.uk
Website: www.ombudsman-wales.org.uk

Royal Air Force (RAF) Benevolent Fund

Provides assistance to current and ex-RAF servicemen and women, and their families. This includes charitable assistance.

67 Portland Place
London W1B 1AR

Helpline: 0800 169 2942
Email: info@rafbf.org.uk
Website: www.rafbf.org

Royal Air Forces Association

Provides advice and support for RAF airmen and women, as well as arranging for short respite breaks for carers and residential and sheltered housing.

1171/2 Loughborough Road
Leicester LE4 5ND

Tel: 0116 266 5224
Email: welfare@rafa.org.uk
Website: www.rafa.org.uk

Royal National Institute for the Blind

Offers information, advice and support for people in the UK who have sight problems.

105 Judd Street
London WC1H 9NE

Helpline: 020 7388 126
Email: helpline@rnib.org.uk
Website: www.rnib.org.uk

Royal National Institute for the Deaf

Campaigns on behalf of people with hearing impairments. It also offers advice, information and support for these people.

19–23 Featherstone Street
London EC1Y 8SL

Helpline: 0808 808 0123
Textphone: 0808 808 9000
Email: informationline@rnid.org.uk
Website: www.rnid.org.uk

Royal Naval Benevolent Trust

Provides financial advice and grants for older people, including supplementing incomes. It also runs a care home specifically for ex-servicemen of the Royal Navy.

Castaway House
311 Twyford Avenue
Portsmouth PO2 8RN

Tel: 023 9269 0112
Email: rnbt@rnbt.org.uk
Website: www.rnbt.org.uk

Relatives and Residents Association

Offers information and support to all involved in long-term care.

24 The Ivories
6–18 Northampton Street
London N1 2HY

Tel: 020 7359 8148
Email: info@relres.org
Website: www.relres.org

Rowan Organisation

A national organisation of disabled people which provides disabled people with access to information, services and resources in order to increase their opportunity for independence and enable them to make informed choices about their future.

Rowan House
Lime Tree Courtyard
Main Road
Ratcliff
Culey CV9 3PD

Tel: 01827 718 972
Website: www.therowan.org

Royal British Legion

A charity offering help to ex-servicemen and women and their families.

48 Pall Mall   LegionLine: 0845 772 5725
London SW1Y 5JY   Website: www.britishlegion.org.uk

Royal British Legion's Ex-Service Homes Referral Agency

Assists in finding a care home placement for an ex-serviceman or woman.

48 Pall Mall   Tel: 020 7839 4466
London SW1Y 5JY   Email: eshra@britishlegion.org.uk

Royal Commonwealth Ex-Services League

Assists ex-servicemen and women through charitable funding.

48 Pall Mall   Tel: 020 7973 7263
London SW1Y 5JY   Email: mgordon-roe@commonwealth
                                 veterans.org.uk
                                 Website: www.bcel.org.uk

Saga Long-Term Care Funding Advice Service

Provides free impartial advice and information about care home fees and funding a place in a care home. It can also advise on long-term insurance policies for care home fees.

Tel: 0800 056 8153   Website: www.saga.co.uk/ltc

Scottish Commission for the Regulation of Care

Responsible for regulating and monitoring care services provided by care homes and home care agencies in Scotland. It can also arrange for the investigation of complaints about these services.

Compass House   Tel: 0845 603 0890
Discovery Quay   Website: www.carecommission.com
11 Riverside Drive
Dundee DD1 4NY

Scottish Executive Central Heating Programme and Warm Deal

Scottish Gas provides this service on behalf of the Scottish Executive. It provides central heating, installation and advice to households where one person or more is aged over 60. It is available to householders who rent from a private landlord or who own their own home.

Tel: 0800 316 6009

Website: www.chwdp-scottish executive.co.uk/index.php

Scottish Independent Advocacy Alliance (SIAA)

SIAA promotes the development of independent advocacy organisations in Scotland. It can help you find local advocacy groups in your area.

Melrose House
69a George Street
Edinburgh EH2 2JG

Tel: 0131 260 5380
Email: enquiry@siaa.org.uk
Website: www.siaa.org.uk

Scottish Public Services Ombudsman

Will consider complaints about public bodies, including the NHS and local government organisations.

Freepost EH641
Edinburgh EH3 0BR

Tel: 0800 377 7330
Email: ask@spso.org.uk
Website: www.scottishombudsman.org.uk

Scottish Veterans Residences

Residential accommodation for ex-servicemen in Scotland. It provides low to medium dependency support in shared homes.

Whiteford House
53 Canongate
Edinburgh EH8 8BS

Tel: 0131 556 0091
Email: info@svronline.org
Website: www.svronline.org

Society of Chiropodists and Podiatrists

Represents practising chiropodists and podiatrists. It can offer foot care advice and advise on locating a local practice.

Head Office
1 Fellmonger's Path
Tower Bridge Road
London SE1 3LY

Tel: 020 7234 8620
Website: www.feetforlife.org

Soldiers, Sailors, Airmen and Families Association (SSAFA)

A national charity helping serving and ex-servicemen, women and their families, including widows and widowers in need. It runs a network of local groups.

19 Queen Elizabeth Street
London SE1 2LP

Tel: 0845 130 0975
Email: info@ssafa.org.uk
Website: www.ssafa.org.uk

Solicitors for the Elderly

A national association of solicitors, barristers and legal executives who provide comprehensive and independent legal advice for older people, their families and carers.

Room 17
Conbar House
Mead Lane
Hertford
Hertfordshire SG13 7AP

Tel: 01992 471 568
Email: jcameron@solicitorsforthe
elderly.com
Website: www.solicitorsforthe
elderly.com

Stroke Association

Funds research into stroke and associated disability. It can provide information about how to cope with a stroke, and it supports carers through community services, information services and welfare grants.

Stroke Information Service
240 City Road
London EC1V 2PR

Helpline: 0845 3033 100
Email: info@stroke.org.uk
Website: www.stroke.org.uk

TaxHelp

This is a charity which provides free advice to older people who cannot afford to pay for financial advice. It can advise about all tax issues affecting older people.

Tel: 0845 601 3321

Third Age Employment Network

Provides signposting for older people looking for work. It can advise about employment, training and career development issues.

207–221 Pentonville Road
London N1 9UZ

Tel: 020 7843 1590
Email: taen@helptheaged.org.uk
Website: www.taen.org.uk

United Kingdom Home Care Association (UKHCA)

The independent representative of providers of domiciliary care. It can provide information about local agencies.

Group House
2nd Floor
52 Sutton Court Road
Sutton
Surrey SM1 4SL

Tel: 020 8288 5291
Website: www.ukhca.co.uk

Veterans Agency

This agency can advise those who were in armed service, as well as their spouses. It can process claims for war pensions and lump sum payments.

Norcross
Blackpool FY5 3WP

Helpline: 0800 169 2277
Tel: 00 44 125 386 6043 (*from overseas*)
Email: help@veteransagency.gsi.gov.uk
Website: www.veteransagency.mod.uk

Victim Support

Provides support for the victims of crime. Regional office details are available on its website, or in your local telephone directory.

Helpline: 0845 303 0900

Email: contact@victimsupport.org.uk
Website: www.victimsupport.org.uk

Vitalise

A national charity which provides holidays for disabled and visually-impaired people. It enables carers to have a break, and also provides opportunities for volunteering.

12 City Forum
250 City Road
London EC1V 8AF

Tel: 0845 345 1972
Website: www.vitalise.org.uk

Volunteer Development Scotland

Provides details of local voluntary projects recruiting volunteers in Scotland.

Stirling Enterprise Park
Stirling FK7 7RP

Tel: 01786 479 593
Email: vds@vds.org.uk
Website: www.vds.org.uk

Volunteering England

This charity can provide details of local voluntary projects recruiting volunteers.

Regents Wharf
8 All Saints Street
London N1 9RL

Tel: 0845 305 6979
Email: information@volunteering
england.org.uk
Website: www.volunteering.org.uk

War Widows' Association

A campaigning organisation which represents war widows and their dependants to ensure better services for those who experience bereavement of someone who served in the Armed Forces and died as a result of this service.

c/o 48 Pall Mall
London SW1Y 5JY

Tel: 0870 241 1305
Website: www.warwidowsassociation.
org.uk

Warm Front

The body which provides grants for heating and insulation improvements in England.

Tel: 0800 316 2805

Email: bec@eaga.com
Website: www.warmfront.co.uk

Winter Fuel Payments Helpline

For information and advice about the Winter Fuel Payments scheme.

Tel: 0845 915 1515

Website: www.thepensionservice.gov.
uk/winterfuel/home.asp

Witness

Advises and supports people who have been abused by health or social care professionals and aims to prevent future abuse.

Delta House
175–177 Borough High Street
London SE1 1HR

Helpline: 0845 450 0300
Email: info@witnessagainstabuse.org.uk
Website: www.popan.org.uk

Women's Royal Voluntary Service

Practical support for older and disabled people.

Garden House
Milton Hill
Steventon
Abingdon OX13 6AD

Tel: 01235 442 900
Website: www.wrvs.org.uk

Index

ElderCare

Week | Promoting care for older people

With the increase in Britain's ageing population, one of the biggest challenges for older people, their families and carers is getting the help and advice they need.

ElderCare Week is an annual event of special activities that aims to highlight the care issues facing older people and how they and their families can get the best advice and plan ahead.

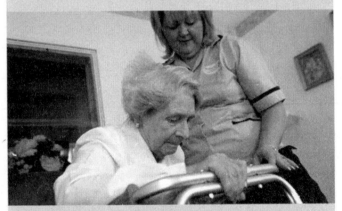

Go to **www.lawpack.co.uk/eldercareweek** or **www.counselandcare.org.uk** to get full details

Sponsored by   counsel+care    **LAWPACK**
for older people, their families and carers